Kierkegaard and Consciousness

Kierkegaard
& Consciousness

BY ADI SHMUËLI

Translated by Naomi Handelman

PRINCETON UNIVERSITY PRESS
PRINCETON, NEW JERSEY

1971

LCC 70-132241
ISBN 0-691-07143-8

This book has been composed in Linotype Baskerville

Translation of this book has been supported
by the Louis A. Robb Fund of Princeton University Press;
and publication has been aided
by Tel-Aviv University and the Whitney
Darrow Publication Reserve Fund of
Princeton University Press

Printed in the United States of America by
Princeton University Press

In memory of my teacher

MESHULAM GROLL

CONTENTS

ACKNOWLEDGMENTS

I WOULD LIKE to express my thanks to Professor Niels Thulstrup and Professor Howard V. Hong for facilitating my work at the Søren Kierkegaard Selskabet in Copenhagen. To Professor Pierre Mesnard and Professor Claude Bruaire of the University of Tours I am grateful for guidance during the writing of this book. I feel especially indebted to Professor Paul L. Holmer of Yale Divinity School and to Mrs. Carol Orr of Princeton University Press for the work they invested in editing this book. Finally, thanks are due to the Research Authority of Tel-Aviv University for its support toward publication.

ADI SHMUËLI

FOREWORD

It is not often in the life of a professional scholar that a manuscript both baffles and attracts. These pages originally came my way couched in the form of a doctoral dissertation from a French university. They were a little unlike most pages of most dissertations; for clearly their author, Mr. Adi Shmuëli, a citizen of Israel, was both convinced in a very strong way that forced consideration of his opinions and was not in the least intimidated (though he seemed amply informed) by the authorities he knew and cited. Though his text was difficult to assimilate as it stood, it exuded strength of thought along with a somewhat brash style. Whether these novelties are enough to make a book is a moot point; for me, in any case, they were not. There were other features that struck me.

What seemed even more surprising and worthy of note was that these pages treated Søren Kierkegaard in a manner quite different than the vast secondary literature which floods the intellectual marketplaces of Europe and America. Here again the author seemed both instructed by that literature, yet rather free to depart from it. His pages concern, as the reader will soon note, the strange business of "human consciousness"; and he dares to construe Kierkegaard's pages as limning as well as stimulating all that makes men conscious.

After some reconsideration and rewriting, the text of this book came forth. This book will perhaps still be baffling for

many readers, but it might also be a stimulus to a deeper
and more exacting grasp of Kierkegaard's texts. Though I
have many difficulties with individual passages in these pages
and though my own proclivities are rather more closely
disciplined by little issues and more care about specific turns
in Kierkegaard's argument, still I have been forced by these
pages to think more assiduously for myself. Perhaps a few
remarks might give the reader a clue to the differences this
volume makes.

First, there is the author's choice of "consciousness" as a
proper subject for study. It is one thing to study the concept,
"consciousness," and quite another to study consciousness
itself. Mr. Shmuëli has studied those philosophers and those
philosophies which are often called phenomenological and
existentialist. His orientation is toward neither historical
studies nor conceptual matters. It is almost as if consciousness itself can be the subject matter. So, he, therefore, with
uncommon boldness, dares to read Kierkegaard's pages as
though they were testimony on consciousness. Kierkegaard
does not quite say so himself; and for an author who was
so rich in a kind of self-analysis, it might seem to be an
omission that was not altogether fortuitous. But again, the
author, emboldened by a philosophical community of our
day, goes ahead on a conviction of his own even where texts
do not quite overtly elicit his kind of analysis.

Despite that fact, however, his metaphysical-like study is
also something else. For Mr. Shmuëli has really let the texts
of Kierkegaard be the subject of his scrutiny. And, therefore,
it is almost as if those very rich comments tend to map out
the concept and all of its powers and capacities within that
literature. So, despite the metaphysical daring of manner,
the logic of the term does become the subject matter of his
essay. It is via that mapping and placing of the concept in
Kierkegaard's discussion of life's stages that "consciousness"

one's own concern and passion, is the condition that all of Kierkegaard's pages showed to be essential to everything noble and truly upbuilding. That this should have become clear and something of an obligation is a tribute to Mr. Shmuëli's abilities and his text.

PAUL L. HOLMER

YALE UNIVERSITY

his pages on consciousness actually more telling because they suggest something else. Surely, Mr. Shmuëli's delineation also makes clear that becoming conscious is not quite an internal activity, not quite one more process taking place in the dim recesses of the mind. It is not so much an activity as it is an achievement in the life history of a man. By using the word "consciousness," the author has highlighted what it means to say that one "understands" this range of things and has also thrown light on Kierkegaard's manifold literature.

Surely it is very difficult to hit the nail on the head. One would not praise this book by claiming too much for it in this respect. But it does seem to me that a certain courage and imagination is required in commentators who address Kierkegaard's pages. Furthermore, the author does not do all of the thinking for his reader. But he has rearranged what so many of us have already read and he has reminded us of what is otherwise forgotten; and he has done this with the help of a philosophical theory. Some will be happy about the former and will discard the latter. Others will perhaps cherish the growing sovereignty of a kind of phenomenology that has now taken the measure of one of its antiheroes.

Such is the boldness of this book, that either might happen. While I might fault the author for not weaning Kierkegaard of those philosophical comments which seem to confuse his pages, Mr. Shmuëli goes intrepidly on, really extending some of the formal philosophical parts of speech that Kierkegaard imparted from the philosophical culture of his day into a twentieth-century philosophical outlook. The fact that I am not convinced is not an indictment of the book, for it does something else very well. In a manner that is often tangential · and even obtuse, it does investigate an aspect of Kierkegaard's authorship that is otherwise neglected.

For to become conscious, to make oneself the object of

begins to gain some clarity for the reader. Saying that something of the grammar of the notion is being done for us is
not too long a step to take here.

But there is something more too. Kierkegaard had thought
a great deal about what it meant to "understand" difficult
matters like Christianity and morals and matters that had to
do with ways and views of life. By using notions of "the
meaning of life" and "truth," all kinds of strange juxtapo-
sitions of human passion and intellectual criteria have continually been celebrated. Kierkegaard tried to rearrange all
of these confusing matters by separating moral and religious
striving for a new quality of life from the pursuit of knowledge about the world, oneself, and even moral and religious
matters. The point was that there were at least two kinds of
interests. But in another way they were also richly intercon-
nected. So, he was at pains to show us that "understanding"
is not always the same as "knowing about" something. The
man who thinks that he understands a moral matter when
he is able to talk or write a book about it, is confusing
"understanding" with an activity like talking or writing. On
the contrary, Kierkegaard "showed" (he did not do a
philosophical theory "about") his pseudonymous figures that
they had room in their lives, genuine capacities, for feeling,
passion, emotion, and interest; and it was in virtue of these
capacities that one could say that they understood.

"Understanding" morals and religion is not, then, a
matter of a more subtle activity, even a philosophical activity, nor is it a matter of even having Kierkegaard's philosophy. Instead, it is not an activity at all; and that is why
Kierkegaard refused to write out his understanding of these
matters. Instead, his literature tries to create that activity
and that capacity that would simply be the understanding.

Though Mr. Shmuëli wants Kierkegaard to be a more
subtle and adequate philosopher than any heretofore, I find

Kierkegaard and Consciousness

INTRODUCTION

THE DIFFICULTIES encountered in studying the philosophy of Kierkegaard—especially in treating it as a coherent whole—are worthy of note, for even those difficulties illumine its nature. In his works, Kierkegaard seems to deploy contradictory ideas which threaten to make his philosophy incomprehensible. For example, Kierkegaard speaks of what he terms "stages" in life—the esthetical (or esthetic), ethical, and religious. The second part of his *Either/Or* deals with the ethical stage in the course of which man makes his choice and comes into his own by choosing freedom. Kierkegaard discusses the ethicist's will, the pathos of the ethical choice, the absolute character of the choice, etc. Reading this text, the student believes that he knows what freedom is all about, and that he has understood Kierkegaard. However, other works show Kierkegaard arguing that man has no freedom of choice at all. He emphasizes several times that the only choice man has before God is to renounce freedom of choice and instead choose to "surrender."[1] The reader interested in the philosophic problem of freedom will certainly find it hard to decide whether man is free or not, according to Kierkegaard. This is one example of Kierkegaard's apparent contradictory manner.

There is another contradiction in his philosophy which is much more fundamental, however, and which challenges the philosophical value of his thinking. Kierkegaard main-

3

tains on numerous occasions that existence and thought are not identical, that existence is transcendent and qualitatively different than thought, and that therefore it cannot be known or thought about. A number of studies, especially that of Paul L. Holmer, have noted this important point; for in maintaining this, Kierkegaard takes particular issue with Hegel's philosophy.[2] What these studies have missed, however, is that Kierkegaard's ideas on existence embody a philosophic contradiction of an internal nature. If consciousness does not encompass existence, if one cannot think about transcendent being, by the same token one cannot know that this being exists; and consequently, neither would one know how to speak of it. To say thinking and being are not identical is to make a statement that is philosophically contradictory. For a suggestion of this kind ostensibly deals with some unknown thing called "existence," or "being," but this thing, since it is unknown, cannot be dealt with in words.

The point is that Kierkegaard is more subtle than this criticism suggests. We are speaking really of a surface reading, the kind of which many commentators are unfortunately guilty. For with an author who wrote a twenty-volume journal and who carefully contrived his authorship and every book in it, it is very unlikely that obvious contradictions would have been long overlooked. In fact, they were not. And it is the purpose of this study to show that these contradictions in the texts were not overlooked, nor are they faults in the philosophical outlook of the author. Instead they are part of the design of that literature, calculated to force a new kind of consciousness upon the reader. That consciousness is actually both the goal of the writings —for Kierkegaard wants to effect a change in his reader— as well as being part of the subject matter of his pages.

4

Therefore, it will be contended that consciousness is a broader concept than the word "thought" might suggest. Thus, when he says that a man cannot "think" existence, he does not mean to say that existence cannot be addressed or that the term lacks all meaning. Because men are conscious in a variety of ways, in virtue of feeling, passion, and other facets of the subjective life, they can assimilate and adapt to the world, even where there are limits of thought and language.*

Questions and contradictions of the kind noted arise frequently in the study of Kierkegaard, and commentators have not resolved their presence. So long as the internal contradictions in Kierkegaard's philosophy are not resolved, it remains incomprehensible as a body of thought; only in reconstituting its internal coherence can its outstanding and even unique importance in the history of philosophy be seen. Scholars have not sufficiently demonstrated this coherence, and it is our opinion that they have been led astray often by Kierkegaard's terminology.**

Kierkegaard uses vernacular language as well as philosophical terms to express his ideas. In general we know, or rather we believe that we know, what the terms "will," "choice," "freedom," etc., mean, and we assume that in using them Kierkegaard intends the same meaning. This assumption is the source of a great deal of misunderstanding, for the terms that Kierkegaard uses do not always have the

---

* Editor's note: It is well to remember that "conscience" in French fairly well covers both what we mean by "conscience" and by "consciousness." It is appropriate to remark, too, that Kierkegaard's concept of "consciousness," when inferred from the whole authorship, as the author does, is broader than that suggested by everyday English usage.

** Editor's note: Note, however, the attempt of Paul Sponheim's book, *Kierkegaard on Christ and Christian Coherence* (New York, 1968), where a kind of coherence is argued at great length.

5

meaning they carry in everyday speech nor even in the lexi-
con of philosophy. Indeed, Kierkegaard himself warns us
against the misleading nature of language. He calls it
"thieves' cant" (Tyvesprog), for language does not always
express our thoughts adequately. Language may distort our
ideas and "steal," i.e., hide, the real meaning of the activity
of our consciousness. Kierkegaard points out that two people may use the same term but for different purposes. Language is deceptive; it is the basis of misunderstanding
between people, and it is responsible for the difficulty
experienced in penetrating the meaning of the Kierkegaard-
ian philosophy. Kierkegaard often uses various terms to
draw attention to what is basically the same thing; for example, the terms "will," "repentance," "despair," "choice,"
"suffering," "culpability," "resignation," "love," can all be
subsumed under the conscious act of negation. On the other
hand, Kierkegaard sometimes uses the same term to designate two totally different things. In his works, the terms
"existence" and "being" sometimes refer to transcendent
reality, and sometimes to the reality of the possible, or of
thought.

Because language serves consciousness in such a variety
of ways, not simply expressing it or giving names to things,
the way we ordinarily think about words can easily deceive
us. Though Kierkegaard does say that language does deceive us, it surely must be that men deceive themselves. It
is not language that is so much at fault as it is the way in
which we construe it. It is speech in the mouths of men that
is faulty, not language all by itself.

Disregarding the ordinary meaning of the terms em-
ployed by Kierkegaard is the first vital step toward success-
fully reestablishing the coherence of his philosophy.* This

* Editor's note: When it is said here and elsewhere that "ordinary
meanings" are being criticized, it ought to be clear that the author is

philosophy is the description of the structure and behavior of human consciousness. The delineation of this structure has provided the key to Kierkegaard's philosophy, and this present work attempts to reconstruct the philosophy by showing that it always reflects the structure in question. It will become clear that Kierkegaard's philosophy, although it deals with being *qua* being, is nevertheless thoroughly nonmetaphysical, and in fact rejects metaphysics as sheer abstraction. Again though, the issue is to show that Kierkegaard has seen that while being cannot be thought, men can be "conscious" with respect to reality.

This study approaches the problems involved as follows: First, human consciousness is analyzed in order to demonstrate that the esthetic, ethical, and religious stages of life are successive steps in the gradual awakening of consciousness. The next chapter is devoted to a description of the alienation of consciousness of which Kierkegaard speaks in all his works. In fact, the aim of Kierkegaard's philosophy is to make the reader aware of this alienation which continually menaces human consciousness. The problem of alienation leads to Kierkegaard's theory of indirect communication, which is the means by which consciousness can be saved from alienation. Everything unique and original in Kierkegaard's philosophy is embodied in this theory. The philosophy as a whole is philosophical action rather than philosophical contemplation, and its importance lies not only in "what" Kierkegaard says, but also in "how" he says it, i.e., in its form. The form is indirect communication, ac-

---

not trespassing at all upon "ordinary language" as this is talked about by recent American and British philosophers. What Kierkegaard is criticizing is usually crudities in cursory and everyday usage. What the recent philosophers are talking about is something quite different, namely, the fact that the meaning of a word can be ascertained only when one looks for its proper and ordered (in this sense "ordinary") use.

tion whose aim it is to awaken consciousness in order to rescue it from alienation. This is also the aim of Christianity, which, according to Kierkegaard, is also an indirect communication.

In studying the observations of Kierkegaard on Christianity as indirect communication, we shall also deal with his reflections on the philosophical problem of truth. Kierkegaard replaces the classical definition of truth with another which is expressed in the famous sentence: "Truth is subjectivity." We shall demonstrate that this sentence is actually a negative definition of truth, and that basically it means that truth is intersubjectivity. According to Kierkegaard, subjectivity cannot be attained except with the help of someone else, and a person becomes a Christian only within a Christian society.

The last chapter of this work deals with the temporality and historicity of human consciousness. It demonstrates that consciousness has a temporal structure, and that each moment of this structure expresses the three dimensions of time simultaneously.

Quotations are generously provided in order to put the reader in direct contact with Kierkegaard's own words. In the main these are taken from English translations of Kierkegaard. Sometimes a word or two is changed to render the original Danish more felicitously; the changed words appear in brackets followed, in most cases, by the Danish words in parentheses. Quotations from works for which no English translations are available have been translated from the texts of *Søren Kierkegaards Samlede Værker* (3rd edition, 1963) and *Søren Kierkegaards Papirer* (2nd edition, 1909-1946).

1.

About Consciousness in General

By the term consciousness we mean what Kierke-gaard called "immanence." This is a general term applying to all conscious human activity, including thoughts, feelings, desires, passions, etc. In Kierkegaard's philosophy, these distinctions lose the independent character they have in ordinary discourse and other philosophies, such as Descartes', for instance. This chapter proposes an independent analysis of the nature of consciousness. It will be seen as we proceed that the confirmation of its correctness can be found in Kierkegaard's works.

In order to describe the features of consciousness, let us consider perception as an analogue of man's conscious thought. Let us imagine a black dot on a white surface. Looking at them, one sees them spatially together and at the same time; and when one concentrates on the black dot, the white surface is relegated to the periphery of the visual field. Conversely, when attention is concentrated on the adjacent surface, it is the black dot that recedes to the periphery. Furthermore, one cannot look steadily for very long at either the dot or the surface, for one's attention alternates involuntarily between the dot and the background, each of which recedes in turn to the periphery of the visual field. This is a fact which Gestalt psychology has pointed out, and which each of us can prove to his own satisfaction. Perception is structured psychological process which provides evi-

dence of the tension that develops between two components, one of them a particular phenomenon, and the other the background upon which the phenomenon appears. This same tension or interplay characterizes every activity of human consciousness.

According to Kierkegaard, man is "a synthesis of the infinite and the finite,"[1] or, as he says in *The Concept of Dread,* a synthesis of the body (that is, of sensuality) and the soul.[2] Human consciousness has two facets which are connected in a dialectical relationship. The finite and the infinite— sensual matter and the soul—are clearly distinguishable in it, negating each other and yet relating to each other. Consciousness is something like the general background upon which a particular phenomenon looms up at any instant. The particular phenomenon is like an item of which one can be conscious; but it is also distinguishable from that context or background of which one is less particularly aware and against which the isolated phenomenon gets its locus and meaning, pertinence and scope. But the self-assertion of the particular phenomenon is also its own negation, for it is consciousness as a background, as a frame of reference, which gives the phenomenon its meaning, by making it appear as one specific phenomenon or another. However, for the phenomenon to have a specific meaning, while standing out it must allow consciousness to assert itself as background. It must not pervade the entire breadth of consciousness, or it will lose the frame of reference provided, and one would no longer be aware of a specific thing that has meaning. Now consciousness seizes a particular phenomenon through a reflective act which is both affirmative and negative, which is carried out and retracted simultaneously, and thus allows itself to be glimpsed at the same time as the background. This act operates so that the emergence

of the phenomenon and its self-assertion as a particular phenomenon is at the same time its own negation, the retraction which permits the appearance of consciousness as the background against which the phenomenon acquires its meaning. A human consciousness, or immanence, is precisely this dialectical tension between the general and the particular, between the infinite and the finite.

The particular phenomenon emerges through the action of a particular and transcendent existence which attacks consciousness from the outside. But existence withdraws and hides at the same time as it gives rise to the particular phenomenon. One is never conscious of it, for the phenomenon whose emergence it causes is always the veil which hides it. When one is conscious of something, that thing as a real being has already disappeared, and the phenomenon is no more than a possibility.

Real and particular existence, or being *qua* being, can never be attained by reflective consciousness, as "being" is always beyond it. Consequently, the phenomenon is a double negation—the negation of consciousness as background, and the negation of transcendent existence. The first negation is not a logical contradiction, but rather a relationship between two dialectical contraries. On the other hand, the second negation is the expression of a purely logical contradiction, for the emergence of the phenomenon *is* the negation and the disappearance of transcendent existence. From the moment of its birth, the phenomenon proves to be the absence or negation of existence. That is why Kierkegaard is opposed to any philosophy which purports to have demonstrated the identification of being and thought. Such an identification would be a logical contradiction, for being and thought, transcendent reality and the domain of the possible, contradict each other logically. The conscious

11

rational transition from consciousness to being *qua* being is a logical impossibility, i.e., a paradox. One cannot therefore identify being with thinking, and according to Kierkegaard the attempts of Descartes and Hegel in this connection only led to the making of tautologies. The being that is thought about is not the actual being, but merely its possible, in other words, a mental being. Saying that being and thinking are identical would be saying that thinking and thinking are identical. As regards the actual being, Kierkegaard's attitude can be summarized as follows: I think, therefore I do not exist. Thought cannot know that an existing thing exists, nor can it prove it. Kierkegaard writes:

> Thus I always reason from existence, not toward existence, whether I move in the sphere of palpable sensible fact or in the realm of thought. I do not for example prove that a stone exists, but that some existing thing is a stone. The procedure in a court of justice does not prove that a criminal exists, but that the accused, whose existence is given, is a criminal. Whether we call existence an *accessorium* or the eternal *prius* it is never subject to demonstration.[3]

Transcendent existence is created by God, and the particular existence of Jesus is its supreme expression. As consciousness cannot know this existence, man needs a religious "leap" with which to clear the fence of consciousness and attain being *qua* being. Only in faith is transcendent reality revealed; no philosophical contemplation and no metaphysics can achieve this reality. The moment of faith reveals that consciousness is a structure that really has three dimensions, namely the two immanent dimensions (the finite and the infinite) on the one hand, and on the other, the transcendent dimension (particular existence) which is the very

origin of consciousness. In the religious stage of life, man becomes a spirit which is "a relation which relates itself to its own self, and in relating itself to its own self relates itself to Another."[4] Consciousness is thus a tripartite relationship joining three dimensions.

However, this chapter has described the structure of consciousness only in its reflective state. Furthermore, consciousness is not such a circumspect and obvious human characteristic as thus far described. For actual people do not always conform to the models that we propose to use in trying to understand them. Kierkegaard has proposed that men, in fact, are usually characterized as behaving esthetically, ethically, and religiously. In these instances, consciousness does not always demonstrate the same structure and characteristics. On the contrary, here we will find actual consciousness sometimes nonreflective, sometimes not aware of itself, and sometimes even alienated from its own nature.

This is why we must turn to his esthetical stage. Here we will begin to discern a more concrete and specific form of consciousness, congruent with a certain manner and style of life. A distinction to be noted later, namely, that between the "how" and the "what" will be delicately appropriate also to the study of consciousness itself.

2.

The Esthetic Consciousness

DURING the romantic or the esthetic stage of life, man is attracted by esthetic ideas. In moments of passion, in heavy moods of melancholy, or the sorrow of nostalgia, the estheticist is caught in a state of mind that resembles a dream. He looks forward to the realization of his poetic ideas, while deep down the sadness of disappointment hovers. He experiences alternately the dizziness of ephemeral enthusiasm, and an undefined lassitude and nonchalance. The estheticist substitutes fantasy for reality. Referring to the pseudonymous author of *Diary of a Seducer*, Kierkegaard writes:

> . . . His poetic temperament . . . is not rich enough, or, perhaps, not poor enough, to distinguish poetry and reality from one another.[1]

In *Either/Or* Judge William provides several descriptions of the estheticist. The structure of consciousness already referred to comes through clearly:

> When an individual regards his self aesthetically he becomes conscious of this self as a manifold concretion very variously characterized; but in spite of the inward diversity, all of it taken together is, nevertheless, his nature, each component has just as much right to assert itself, just as much right to demand satisfaction. His soul is like a plot of ground in which all sorts of herbs are planted, all

14

with the same claim to thrive; his self consists of this mul-
tifariousness, and he has no self which is higher than
this.²

The mind of the estheticist is no more than the tension
between consciousness as background and a particular phenomenon, both of which seek to express themselves at the
same time. This is shown even more clearly in a description
given by Constantius, the pseudonymous author of *Repetition*, who says:

> Surely there is no young man with any imagination who
> has not at one time been captivated by the enchantment
> of the theater, and desired to be himself carried away
> into the midst of that fictitious reality in order to see and
> hear himself as an *alter ego*, to disperse himself among
> the innumerable possibilities which diverge from himself,
> and yet in such a way that every diversity is in turn a sin-
> gle self. Of course it is only at a very early age such a de-
> sire can express itself. Only the imagination is awake to
> this dream of personality, all the other faculties are still
> sound asleep. In such a dream of imagination the individ-
> ual is not a real figure but a shadow, or rather the real
> figure is invisibly present and therefore is not content
> with casting one shadow, but the individual has a multi-
> plicity of shadows, all of which resemble him and for the
> moment have an equal claim to be accounted himself.
> The personality is not yet discovered, its energy an-
> nounces itself only in the passion of possibility; for it is
> true in the life of the spirit as it is in the case of many
> plants that the germinal sprout comes last.³

The estheticist is a multiplicity of possibilities and at the
same time a single possibility. But the ego as actual existence is "invisibly present," and "not yet discovered." Tran-

scendent existence hides behind "the shadow," behind the particular phenomenon which it projects. We therefore know only the particular phenomenon, the projected thing, and never the agent who projects. Transcendent and particular existence is the "germinal sprout" which must come last, or "the real figure" which is not the limited projection of one shadow, but rather "a multiplicity of shadows." Transcendent existence cannot be reduced to phenomena; the particular phenomenon and our entire consciousness will always be a diminution and impoverishment of its vigor. Any identification of consciousness and existence, of thinking and being, which rationalists (be they Hegel, Descartes, or Spinoza) maintain, is no more than an empty abstraction according to Kierkegaard.[4]

As a matter of fact, the words of Constantius that have been cited are an expression of the central philosophical problem that concerned Kierkegaard and motivated his philosophical writings. In consciousness, which contends only with the ephemeral, the changing, and the relative, Kierkegaard also sought the permanent and absolute. Like Pascal, he sought the fixed "persona" beyond man's ephemeral qualities, namely the "seed in the onion" or, as he says, "the germinal sprout that comes last." In his books, he apparently wants to tell the reader that reflective consciousness will never reach this "seed," and that man's real ego can only be achieved through the religious movement that he calls "leap" or "repetition."

Each particular phenomenon is, as has been seen, a double negation of consciousness as a whole and of transcendent existence. The first negation demarcates the impossibility of realizing the totality of consciousness in a single phenomenon, and the second marks the impossibility of the transition from the phenomenon to existence. Thus, being

only a negation, the particular phenomenon has no substantiality, and consciousness appears to be a constant evanescence. Man therefore experiences a painful feeling of failure, as described in *Repetition*. Constantius tells the story of a young man tormented by the fact that the whole of his love and his romantic dreams cannot be realized in the particular image of the young woman he loves. The young man seeks "repetition," which can lead him to transcendent existence. Constantius, too, seeks this repetition, but naturally, does not find it. No immanent activity, whether it be romantic dreaming or philosophical contemplation like that of Constantius, can ever attain transcendent existence. Let us examine the words of Constantius:

> The dialectic of repetition is easy; for what is repeated has been, otherwise it could not be repeated, but precisely the fact that it has been gives to repetition the character of novelty. When the Greeks said that all knowledge is recollection they affirmed that all that is has been; when one says that life is repetition one affirms that existence which has been now becomes. When one does not possess the categories of recollection or of repetition the whole of life is resolved into a void and empty noise. Recollection is the pagan life-view, repetition is the modern life-view; repetition is the *interest* of metaphysics, and at the same time the interest upon which metaphysics founders; repetition is the solution contained in every ethical view, repetition is a *conditio sine qua non* of every dogmatic problem.[5]

> Repetition and recollection are the same movement, only in opposite directions; for what is recollected has been, is repeated backwards, whereas repetition properly so called is recollected forwards.[6]

Kierkegaard deals with repetition by comparing it to the Platonic theory of recollection. Repetition should lead us to the ontological basis of the phenomena, just as recollection purports to do. It is a question then of being *qua* being, since Constantius states explicitly: "If God himself had not willed repetition, the world would never have come into existence."[7]

Nevertheless, Constantius does not believe, nor does Kierkegaard, that being can be attained by recollection:

Hope is a charming maiden but slips through the fingers, recollection is a beautiful old woman but of no use at the instant, repetition is a beloved wife of whom one never tires. . . . It requires youth to hope, and youth to recollect, but it requires courage to will repetition.[8]

Constantius views recollection as simple nostalgia, and he deprives it of the metaphysical importance attached to it by Plato. Recollection, like hope, is only dreaming, and while dreaming one is always within the limits of consciousness which do not encompass being. Repetition is therefore neither a backward movement (toward the past) nor a movement toward the future. Constantius says that it is "daily bread which satisfies with benediction." Repetition thus belongs to the present, and is "recollected forwards." By repetition, one advances forwards, for one must pierce the veil of immanence in order to attain existence which is directly ahead, hidden behind the current phenomenon. What is repeated has been; existence always appears to us as "having already been," since it is vanquished by the very phenomenon which it gives rise to in us. Repetition is thus a religious movement which attains the being that is continually escaping us. Constantius says that "repetition is the interest of metaphysics, and at the same time the interest

upon which metaphysics founders." Metaphysics is no more than a conscious reflective activity, and as such it can never exceed the limits of consciousness. Only the religious leap can do this, and as Constantius is a reflective person lacking faith, he remains tied to the domain of immanence which does not encompass being. He admits that he has failed in his search and has not achieved being:

> Repetition is too transcendent for me also. I can circumnavigate myself, but I cannot erect myself above myself, I cannot find the Archimedean point.[9]

Let us see what goes on within Constantius. He visits Berlin for the second time and arrives carrying the memories of his first visit with him. His images do not belong to the dead past, but rather to a past that is relived and transformed into the present. And this very present is also the expectation of seeing the city. One can imagine him arriving in the city. He quickly seeks his former quarters; he finds them and stands contemplating them. Then he opens the door. He goes up the stairs. Perhaps he starts up slowly and then speeds up, and he eventually reaches the room he formerly lived in. But Constantius is disappointed.

The particular things he now sees deploy themselves against the general background of his recollections, his hopes, his regrets, in brief, against the totality of his present consciousness. Consequently this manifold cannot be realized in a single thing. On the contrary, it is precisely the particular thing which demonstrates the frustration of this realization, since it negates it. In examining his room, Constantius indeed experiences this frustration, and tells us:

> My writing-table was in the accustomed place. The velvet armchair still existed. But when I saw it I was so exasperated that I was near breaking it to bits—all the more

because everybody in the house had gone to bed, and there was no one to take it away. What is the good of a velvet armchair when the rest of the environment doesn't correspond with it? It is as if a man were to walk naked wearing a cocked hat. . . . when I got up next morning I carried into effect my resolution and had it thrown into a store-room.[10]

It is by the negation of a particular thing (the repudiation of the armchair) that the totality of consciousness is confirmed. Constantius strolls through the streets, glances at the cafés and the theatres. The totality of his memories is awakened precisely when he stands before each familiar object. The scope and power of memory are demonstrated in the presence of a particular thing. But this power is demonstrated *through* the particular thing, in other words, by being negated. It is a living power which is revealed by its death; the positive is confirmed by the negative. It is precisely in the current absence of a pleasant past, and the consequent regret felt that its extent and beauty are reflected. And this presence divulged by absence characterizes the continual disappointment of our life. Constantius declares this when he says:

The older one grows and the more understanding of life one acquires, and taste for the agreeable and ability to relish it, in short, the more competent one becomes, the less one is content. Content—entirely and absolutely and in every way content—one never becomes, and to be tolerably content is not worth the trouble, so it is better to be entirely discontented.[11]

The older one is, the more disappointed one becomes. The maturity and power of the mind appear in full force

just when they are eclipsed. Constantius is no longer young; he is experienced and knowledgeable about life. But man's maturity is like starlight. The brighter it is, the more it implies the retreat of the sun which has withdrawn and set, and is no longer visible. Constantius remains confined within the limits of his immanence, where he is constantly wavering between the agitated possibilities of his soul, symbolized by the "post-horn."[12] Repetition is an impossible movement for him, for he is not a believer and therefore does not attain transcendent existence (the Archimedean point) although he knows that it is God who wills repetition, on which the existence of the world depends. Without an ontological basis, without being *qua* being, the world would collapse.

Observations on the character of Constantius have indicated something of the structure of consciousness. The immanence of the estheticist is the tension between a particular phenomenon and consciousness as a whole, and this is seen also in the description of the second character in *Repetition*. In analyzing the character of a young man, Constantius tells us:

> He has retained an ideal conception of the whole love affair, to which he is able to give any expression whatever, but [always in the realm of mood] (altid i Stemning), because he possesses no factual [realm] (Facticitet). He has therefore a fact of consciousness, or rather he has no fact of consciousness but a dialectical elasticity which will make him productive in the realm of [mood].[13]

The immanence of a young man embodies only "facts of consciousness" and is no more than a "dialectic elasticity." The young man is in love with a young woman, and he has no knowledge of her real existence, only of her appearance:

21

So again the girl is not a reality but a reflection of the movements within him and their exciting cause. The girl has a prodigious importance, he actually will never be able to forget her, but what gives her importance is not herself but her relation to him. She is as it were the boundary of his being. But such a relation is not erotic.[14]

When the young man thinks about the young woman, when he sees her or dreams about her, he has only the appearance of her. The actual existence of the young woman which "excites" the apparitions and from which they emerge remains hidden to him. Furthermore, each particular phenomenon is nothing more than the negation of the totality of the young man's poetic consciousness, and he can marry the young woman only at the risk of losing and negating this totality. It is the particular phenomenon which must be dissipated if one wishes to retain the poetic totality. Speaking of the relationship between the young man and the young woman, Constantius says: "She had meant much to him, she had made him a poet, and thereby she had signed her own death warrant."[15]

The young man's love is not realized. He experiences only the flux of evanescent phenomena which hide existence from him. He lacks the fixed and solid root of the phenomenon, namely being. Is it surprising then that he feels as much a stranger to himself as to the world?

My life has been brought to an *impasse,* I loathe existence, it is without savor, lacking salt and sense. . . . One sticks one's finger into the soil to tell by the smell in what land one is: I stick my finger into existence—it smells of nothing. Where am I? . . . What is this thing called the world? What does this word mean? Who is it that has lured me into the thing, and now leaves me there? Who am I? How did I come into the world?[16]

The young man attempts to carry out the movement of repetition, and believes he has accomplished this by identifying himself with Job. Constantius explains that the young man has nonetheless not carried out the true movement of repetition, since he experiences merely a religious feeling.[17] Only the believer can achieve the religious leap, and the young man is merely a romanticist. We note that Kierkegaard himself possibly experienced the same feelings as the young man. In the *Journals* he writes: "If I had had faith, I would have stayed with Regina."[18]

This chapter has considered several passages that clearly describe the dialectic tension of consciousness. It should be noted, however, that these descriptions are delineated by Constantius or by Judge William, who is an ethicist. The first, Constantius, evinces a reflective attitude, for he observes himself while observing and describing the character of the young romanticist. He represents a higher stage in esthetic life, and indeed he is bordering upon the ethical stage which is characterized by reflection, as will be seen subsequently. Reflection is consciousness of oneself, and it is in reflection that man becomes conscious of the dialectic tension of his immanence, and this, consequently permits one to describe its nature. A man living in the esthetic stage is not always a reflective man, and in most cases the estheticist is not aware of the structure of his consciousness, which seems to lack any clear delineation between the general and the particular. The consideration of another description of this dialectical tension may clarify the point better. In *Either/Or*, Kierkegaard speaks of the idea of Don Juan in Mozart's opera, an idea which is the artistic expression of the esthetic life. The idea is described as follows:

> Don Juan constantly hovers between being the idea, that is to say, energy, life—and being the individual. . . . So

23

Don Juan is [an image which] constantly appears, but [which] does not gain form and substance, an individual who is constantly being formed, but who is never finished, whose life history one is no more sensible of, than one is of listening to the tumult of the waves.[19]

The idea of Don Juan, being an expression of esthetic experience, gives evidence of the same dialectical tension between the general and the particular which characterizes consciousness. We note, however, that only Kierkegaard, the reflective author, is conscious of Don Juan's dialectics and reveals its development to us. Don Juan himself, or rather a man who lives in the present like Don Juan, knows nothing about it. Only the reflective man is conscious, in his esthetic experiences, of the dialectics of immanence. The consciousness of an unreflective (immediate) person is, on the contrary, in a state of obscure generality without articulation most of the time; its two dimensions, the general and the particular, are blurred and indistinguishable from each other, as is clearly demonstrated in melancholy, for example, which is a characteristic trait of the immediate esthetic life:

What, then, is melancholy? It is hysteria of the spirit. There comes a moment in a man's life when his immediacy is, as it were, ripened and the spirit demands a higher form in which it will apprehend itself as spirit. Man, so long as he is immediate spirit, coheres with the whole earthly life, and now the spirit would collect itself, as it were, out of this dispersion and become in itself transformed, the personality would be conscious of itself in its eternal validity. If this does not come to pass, if the movement is checked, if it is forced back, melancholy ensues. . . . There is something inexplicable in melancholy. The

man who has sorrow and anxiety knows why he is sorrowful or anxious. If a melancholy man is asked what ground he has for it, what it is that weighs upon him, he will reply, "I know not. I cannot explain it." Herein lies the infinity of melancholy.[20]

A melancholy man is not aware of any definite cause which produces his depressive state. His immanence provides no such articulation, for it has rather produced in him a fusion of consciousness, including the particular and the general in one. His consciousness has become mood-like, resembling an empty abstraction that the following text describes very clearly. The estheticist in *Either/Or*, who is melancholy as well, tells us:

> The result of my life is simply nothing, a mood, a single color. My result is like the painting of the artist who was to paint a picture of the Israelites crossing the Red Sea. To this end, he painted the whole wall red, explaining that the Israelites had already crossed over, and that the Egyptians were drowned.[21]

A well-marked characteristic of the esthetic life is the tendency to become volatilized in imaginary dreams. It even seems as if immanence loses one of its dimensions, since the estheticist experiences only the totality of his consciousness, and is not aware of the particular phenomenon, i.e., of the finite. In his letter to the estheticist, Judge William writes:

> Theoretically you are through with the world, finiteness cannot subsist before your thought; practically you are through with it to a certain degree, that is, in an esthetic sense. Nevertheless, you have no world view, you have something which resembles a view, and this gives your

25

life a certain composure, which must not, however, be confounded with a secure and refreshing confidence in life.[22]

Nevertheless, finiteness, i.e., the finite phenomenon, does not disappear entirely. It still exists, but only as a factor which can only be exterior and strange to consciousness. The estheticist does not consider the finite to be an essential trait of his own immanence, but rather an event which comes from outside and serves only to awaken a state of mind, a mood in him. The finite as such does not interest him, and he only likes experiencing the infinite in his imagination. When he is in love, he is more in love with love than with a single woman, and when he is melancholy, he only knows that he is, and no more. What is missing in his moods is the transitive relations, the relating of mood "to," "of," and "for" this person or that event. However, the estheticist cannot do without the finite. As has already been noted the totality of consciousness awakens only when confronting each individual finite object. In order to experience love, joy, or amusement, a person needs finite events and occasions. He must make his thought, his mood, his feelings, transitive. He is therefore, willy-nilly, joined to the finite, which affects him from outside. Judge William notes:

> But he who says that he wants to enjoy life always posits
> a condition which either lies outside the individual or is
> in the individual in such a way that it is not posited by
> the individual himself.[23]

The tension between the particular and the general which characterizes human consciousness appears in the esthetic stage as a conflicting but on the other hand dependent relationship between the romantic soul and the external

and finite reality. When the latter seems confining, the estheticist constantly attempts to free himself from the yoke
of the finite. He fears that a friend, a wife, or a government
assignment may keep him enslaved.[24] He wants everything
psychological to be intransitive. He wants to live in his
dreams or transform them into his reality. But one way or
another, he still is subject to the finite, and this gives rise to
the feeling of constraint which he constantly experiences.
It seems to him that the world is choking him and he cannot
escape, and that he has nothing to look forward to except
frustration and weariness:

> I feel as if I were a piece in a game of chess, when my
> opponent says of it: That piece cannot be moved.[25]

> Alas, the doors of fortune do not open inward, so that by
> storming them one could force them open; but they open
> outward, and therefore nothing can be done.[26]

Several sorts of esthetic experiences have been considered, and it has been noted that the character of Constantius expresses a developed level of the esthetic stage. He
differs from other estheticists in the Kierkegaard literature
in that he considers the particular phenomenon to be an
internal determinant of consciousness, and not a foreign
and external event. What we have here is an internalization
of the dialectical tension between the particular and the
general. Kierkegaard's philosophy is, thus, also a history of
the awakening of consciousness, and it is obvious that this
awakening begins the moment consciousness is aware of the
finite as such. As a reflective person, Constantius does not
get lost in the detached sequence of endless dreams. He is
completely aware of the immanent tension between the particular and the general, and he is capable of describing its

development. Furthermore, he knows that the meaning of each particular phenomenon is set in the light of the general background of consciousness, and that for this reason alone, the finite can never have one definite meaning. Against the vast panorama of consciousness, anything that we experience in particular can have only appearances that are subject to change. The immanent powers of a man encompass only the possible, and never the real; only the relative and never the absolute. Constantius is aware of this, and as he is incapable of reaching repetition, he says:

Farewell, farewell, thou rich hope of youth! Why dost thou hasten so impetuously? What thou art chasing does not exist, and thou thyself just as little. Farewell, thou manly strength! Why dost thou paw the ground so fiercely? That on which thou treadest is a vain imagination. Farewell, thou victorious purpose! Thou art near enough to the goal, for thou canst not take thy works with thee without turning back, and that thou canst not do. Farewell, farewell delight of the forest! When I desired to see thee thou wast withered. Ride on thou fleeting river! Thou alone dost know what thou wilt, thou who has only the desire to run and lose thyself in the sea, which never becomes full. Go on thou spectacle upon the stage of life, which no one calls a comedy, no one a tragedy, because no one knows the end! Thou theater of existence where life is not given back to one any more than money is! Why did no one ever return from the dead? Because life does not know how to captivate as death does, because life does not possess the power of persuasion which death possesses.[27]

Once a person is conscious of relativity in life, he becomes *eo ipso* aware of the dialectic tension in immanence.

He no longer rushes to lose himself in dreams and delusions. Life, Constantius tells us (and by life he means immediate esthetic life as well as the life of the reflective man), is not as persuasive as death. What is then the point of disguising this fact by hiding behind the romantic metamorphosing of an unbridled imagination? Constantius is ripe for ethical metamorphosis because he is on the threshold of despair. For despair is the turning point between the esthetic and the ethical stage; and one despairs as soon as one is aware of the fact that esthetic immanence encompasses only the possibles and never the real. Man then experiences an internal change in the course of which immanence acquires an ethical meaning. Note, however, that it is not the sort of change which erases and negates what was present in consciousness up to now. The ethical choice of which Kierkegaard speaks is rather an intensification of the determinants of consciousness which takes place when the latter becomes conscious of itself. Kierkegaard writes:

> By the absolute choice the ethical is always posited, but from this it does not follow by any means that the esthetical is excluded. In the ethical the personality is concentrated in itself, so the esthetical is absolutely excluded or is excluded as the absolute, but relatively it is still left. In choosing itself the personality chooses itself ethically and excludes absolutely the esthetical, but since it is itself it chooses and since it does not become another being by choosing itself, the whole of the esthetical comes back again in its relativity.[28]

The next chapter will show that the ethical stage points to the same structure of consciousness which Constantius has begun to describe in *Repetition*. Like Constantius, the ethicist is entirely aware of the two dimensions of con-

sciousness. In choosing the ethical, one chooses oneself and
the dialectical tension by letting the constitutive element be
clearly stated. The ethicist William tells us:

> My either/or does not in the first instance denote the
> choice between good and evil, it denotes the choice
> whereby one chooses good *and* evil/or excludes them.
> Here the question is under what determinants one would
> contemplate the whole of existence and would himself
> live. That the man who chooses good and evil chooses the
> good is indeed true, but this becomes evident only after-
> wards; for the esthetical is not the evil but neutrality, and
> that is the reason why I affirmed that it is the ethical
> which constitutes the choice.[29]

The choice is between good and evil on the one hand, and
indifference on the other hand. On one side we have the
clear distinction between the particular phenomenon and
consciousness as a general background; on the other is the
abstract character of any romantic dream. The choice,
therefore, lies between the articulation of the components
that make up one's personality or continuing to keep them
in abeyance, almost in an abstract and intransitive relation.

3.

The Ethical Consciousness

In *Either/Or,* Judge William frequently indicates that the transition from the esthetical to the ethical stage is an absolute choice through which one chooses oneself. To be conscious now requires that one have a transitive relation to oneself. He emphasizes that this choice embodies as well a characteristic dialectic:

> In this case choice performs at one and the same time two dialectical movements: that which is chosen does not exist and comes into existence with the choice; that which is chosen exists, otherwise there would not be a choice. For in case what I chose did not exist but absolutely came into existence with the choice, I would not be choosing, I would be creating; but I do not create myself, I choose myself. Therefore, while nature is created out of nothing, while I myself as an [immediate] personality am created out of nothing, as a free spirit I am born of the principle of contradiction, or born by the fact that I choose myself.[1]

Although a level of consciousness already exists, it is created anew during the ethical stage, and establishes itself via an *"either/or"* which is engendered by the principle of contradiction. The choice in question is no more than man's consciousness of himself, or the awakening of consciousness whereby it becomes aware of its own determinants, in other words, of the fact that it augments the tension between the

general and the particular. We have seen that during the esthetic stage, man either is oblivious of the finite, or tries to free himself from it since it appears to him to be an external and inhibiting element. The estheticist would like to become etherealized in the abstractions and romantic dreams that intoxicate him. But in this flight, he is doubly tied to the immediate, or rather, he himself is immediate in a double sense. On the one hand, he identifies himself positively and immediately with romantic abstractions, and on the other hand, he is riveted to the finite, whether he likes it or not. In both cases, he is at the mercy of chance which must provide him with propitious occasions for experiencing ephemeral joy or enthusiasm. Because he is the slave of chance, the immediate looms up for him as fortuitous and "created out of nothing," and he feels superfluous and strange in the world. As the young man of *Repetition* says:

> I stick my finger into existence—it smells of nothing. Where am I? . . . What is this thing called the world? What does this word mean? Who is it that has lured me into the thing, and now leaves me there? Who am I?[2]

The estheticist loses himself in the immediate or, what is the same in the end, he is himself a fact that is immediate, fortuitous, and without *raison d'être*.

> The esthetical in a man is that by which he is immediately what he is; the ethical is that whereby he becomes what he becomes.[3]

What characterizes consciousness in the esthetic stage of life is thus its positive nature. In every case it is what it is, i.e., always a positive and final fact. As we shall later observe, positivity is the basic feature of the alienated consciousness. This positivity distinguishes it from the non-

alienated that is never a final and completed fact, but on the contrary is a perpetual movement or process of becoming. Once freed from the illusory substantiality of the romantic world, man comes back, in the ethical stage, to reality and to its articulate diversity:

> Here I would recall the definition I gave a while ago of the ethical, as that by which a man becomes what he becomes. The ethical then will not change the individual into another man but makes him himself, it will not annihilate the esthetical but transfigures it. It is essential to a man who is to live ethically that he become so radically conscious of himself that no adventitious trait escapes him. This concretion the ethical would not obliterate but it sees in this its task, it sees what it has to build upon and what it has to build.[4]

No "adventitious trait" escapes the ethicist. As soon as one is in the ethical stage of life, consciousness acquires control of itself and learns in awakening that the finite belongs to it incontrovertibly. But the finite phenomenon of which the ethicist is conscious never appears as a positive or completed fact, but always as a relative and particular aspect of reality that is at once negated and transcended by the totality of consciousness where it gains meaning. Negativity is what characterizes the nonalienated human consciousness that first develops in the ethical stage of life. Every determinant of consciousness is then expressed by its own negation. The totality of consciousness is not seen as a positive determinant but rather as a lack that is confirmed by the particular phenomenon. On the other hand, the particular phenomenon is not a positive determinant either, since it is the negation of the totality of consciousness. In the ethical stage of life, consciousness is never exhaustively realized in

33

a positive and completed fact, and man never becomes a definite "given" as does a stone or a chair. Being constantly in the process of becoming, he is always ahead of himself,— a task which always remains not yet accomplished.

In the second volume of *Either/Or*, the ethicist, Judge William, tries to persuade the estheticist to choose the ethical life by giving his despair and repentance a direct object. Despair, repentance, and choice are partially overlapping in Kierkegaard's language because they signify the negative character of conscious activity. Whoever chooses to despair or to repent chooses the process of becoming which characterizes the ethical life. One makes oneself one's own object of concern; and, thereby, the self comes into existence:

> Let us now for once compare an ethical and an esthetical individual. The principal difference, and one on which everything hinges, is that the ethical individual is transparent to himself and does not live *ins Blaue hinein* as does the esthetical individual. This difference states the whole case. He who lives ethically has seen himself, knows himself, penetrates with his consciousness his whole concretion, does not allow indefinite thoughts to potter about within him, nor tempting possibilities to distract him with their jugglery; he is not like a witch's letter from which one sense can be got now and then another, depending upon how one turns it. He knows himself.[5]

The ethicist repents of the diversity of his consciousness at the same time that he reattaches himself to it. In other words, the ethical consciousness is a diversity in which each element establishes itself while negating itself. Insofar as it is the emergence of finite content in consciousness, the particular phenomenon is a choice, but it is precisely in repent-

ing, i.e., in detaching oneself, that one also chooses the finite and latches on to it. The positive is confirmed by the negative, and choice is acquired through repentance. Judge William insists:

> I cannot often enough repeat the proposition, however simple it may be in itself, that choosing oneself is identical with repenting oneself. For upon this everything turns. . . . The truly concrete choice is that wherewith at the very same instant I choose myself out of the world I am choosing myself back into the world. For when I choose myself repentantly I gather myself together in all my finite concretion, and in the fact that I have thus chosen myself out of the finite I am in the most absolute continuity with it.[6]

Although the ethicist is aware of the emerging finite, he does not attach himself to it positively. To attach oneself directly and positively is to become a finite, positive, and fortuitious fact oneself, lacking any continuity with other facts. Man would then be led to believe that "the world begins with him," and that "he creates himself." But this is not quite true of the ethicist. It is actually by leaving the world, by repenting, that he chooses to enter it. Consciousness spontaneously absorbs phenomena as soon as the current phenomenon is negated. In the ethical consciousness, the finite is confirmed by its negation, and thereby establishes its relationship and continuity with consciousness as background. Nothing finite escapes the ethical consciousness, and everything finite finds in it the continuity and frame of reference which give it meaning.

The relationships between the finite and consciousness as background are the constituents of the individual's history. Every finite enters into a relationship with other finite facts already located in consciousness:

The man we are speaking of discovers now that the self he chooses contains an endless multiplicity, inasmuch as it has a history, a history in which he acknowledges identity with himself. This history is of various sorts; for in this history he stands in relation to other individuals of the race and to the race as a whole, and this history contains something painful, and yet he is the man he is only in consequence of this history. Therefore, it requires courage for a man to choose himself; for at the very time when it seems that he isolates himself most thoroughly he is most thoroughly absorbed in the root by which he is connected with the whole. This alarms him, and yet so it must be, for when the passion of freedom is aroused in him (and it is aroused by the choice, as also it is presupposed in the choice) he chooses himself and fights for the possession of this object as he would for his eternal blessedness; and it is his eternal blessedness. He cannot relinquish anything in this whole, not the most painful, not the hardest to bear, and yet the expression for this fight, for this acquisition is . . . repentance. He repents himself back into himself, back into the family, back into the race, until he finds himself in God.[7]

By repenting, the ethical man becomes himself and his neighbor at the same time, i.e., himself and his social environment. This clarifies the behavior of consciousness in which each phenomenon is simultaneously both itself and also that consciousness which is antecedent and foundational. The family or the race in question are equivalent to this background, i.e., they are possibles and potentials in consciousness. Kierkegaard in *Postscript* emphasizes that one knows one's fellow man only as a possibility, and never as actual reality.[8] The following excerpt from the *Journals* further elucidates this point:

Is the historical then not reality? Certainly. But what history? The history of six thousand years of the world is certainly reality, but a past reality. For me it is and can only be a reality which is thought, i.e., a possibility. Whether the dead really fulfilled the duties which were set them existentially or not is now decided once and for all. To them there is now no longer any existential reality except in the past and that past, once again, only exists for one as ideal reality, as reality in thought, as possibility.[9]

The other man, whether living or dead, is only a possible in consciousness. The ethicist is aware of this, for he is simultaneously himself and his social fundament. The relationship which the ethicist maintains with his fellow man and with his history expresses itself anew when Judge William says that the ethicist is a "universal man":

> The task which the ethical individual sets himself is to transform himself into the universal man. . . . But to transform oneself into the universal man is only possible if already *kata dunamin* I have this in myself. . . . In the act of despair the universal man comes forth and now is behind the concretion, breaking out through it. . . . Every man can, if he will, become the paradigmatic man, not by wiping out his accidentality but by remaining in it and ennobling it. But he ennobles it by choosing it.[10]

The universal man is "in myself," that is, in my very consciousness, as the potentiation, which is realized only by the negation of the finite, i.e., in this case by a kind of renunciation. The act of despair is equivalent to the act of repentance, or, in other words, the act of choice. All these terms express something of the same idea, namely, that of the negation of the finite phenomenon. Kierkegaard also uses

the term "action" to emphasize the active aspect of this negation which constantly develops in the consciousness of the ethicist. He writes:

> The ethical individual knows himself, but this knowledge is not a mere contemplation (for with that the individual is determined by his necessity), it is a reflection upon himself which itself is an action, and therefore I have deliberately preferred to use the expression "choose oneself" instead of know oneself.[11]

The reflective consciousness does not confine itself to the finite phenomenon but while grasping it, at the same time frees itself of it. This consciousness is not "a mere contemplation" (i.e., immediate consciousness), but rather "a reflection upon oneself" (i.e., an action). It is a thinking about, not just thinking. For example, the contemplation of the question of one's death is an action according to Kierkegaard.[12] Consciousness "acts" when it realizes that the finite world may one day be annihilated, that it is precarious. Contemplation of death only enhances the reflective attitude of consciousness during which it detaches itself from the finite. The term "action" then has the same meaning as the terms "choice," "repentance," and "despair": they all refer to the reflective action of consciousness, which detaches itself from the phenomenon while grasping it. And the same thing is true of the term "will" as used by Kierkegaard.

European rationalism, along with most philosophical psychologies, has tended to specify the will in man as one more faculty among others. Descartes considered will a faculty distinct from the faculties of consciousness, and Rousseau, along with most German idealists, retained and developed this idea. The man in the street as well is used to speaking of will, and he is sure that he is endowed with

will just as he is endowed with eyes, arms, etc. In the same way, freedom of choice is discussed and man is imagined as a judge seated some distance away from the possibles, examining them, eventually deciding upon one of them, and attaching his will to it. Kierkegaard holds a different opinion. All of these capacities for him can become transitive and their transitivity is what makes them a part of consciousness.

In speaking of the ethical choice by which one chooses oneself, Judge William says:

> But what, then, is this self of mine? If at the first instant I were to give the first expression for this, my answer is: It is the most abstract of all things, and yet at the same time it is the most concrete—it is freedom.[13]

The freedom in question is what Kierkegaard calls "the choice of surrender":

> Freedom (freedom of choice) exists only in its infinite haste . . . to simultaneously join itself unconditionally to the choice of surrender, a choice of which the truth is that there can be no question of choice.[14]

It is never a matter of choosing between two finite phenomena. We have already seen that the ethicist cannot renounce an "adventitious trait" since it is himself. The emergence of the finite is a bald fact—one meets up with the finite, willy-nilly. However, the ethical man, as opposed to the estheticist, does not attach himself in a positive fashion to the finite, for each finite thing negates itself in him while emerging in order to express the totality of consciousness. Thus, this negation of the finite is actually man's free act. Freedom is choosing resignation or surrender, i.e., carrying out the act of negation, and thereby setting oneself apart

from the finite world. In *Fear and Trembling* Kierkegaard emphasizes the point that resignation is a choice that each person can make if he so desires.[15] Every individual is free to say no to the finite, to choose it while at the same time repenting of it. It is man's prerogative to choose between perdition in the finite and freedom. The latter is established by the very act of surrender, which is actually surrendering to God. In the following chapter we shall see that according to Kierkegaard, the finite world is the continual creation of God. And before God, the only freedom man has is the choice of surrender. Kierkegaard writes:

> A Christian is a man of will who does not want his will any more, but who, with the passion of his own broken (completely changed) will, desires the will of Another.[16]

Kierkegaard uses everyday language but the ordinary meanings are somewhat modified. Will shares, then, a likeness with the reflective act of consciousness that grasps the phenomenon while rejecting it. God creates the world, and man finds himself forced to absorb the finite that emerges in his consciousness. But if man has this "passion of his broken will," in other words, if he rejects the finite, he will thereby become free to absorb another, which God will reveal to him, and which will enrich his consciousness. Through surrender, his consciousness becomes available and free to accept the richness of finite phenomena. Freedom, or the choice of surrender, is the opening of consciousness, its coming-out-of-itself toward phenomena. According to Kierkegaard, this freedom is also the good:

> The good cannot be defined. The good is freedom. The first distinction between good and evil is for and in freedom, and this distinction is never *in abstracto* but always

in concreto. . . . . The distinction between good and evil certainly exists for freedom, but not *in abstracto.* The misunderstanding at this point is due to the fact that freedom is commonly conceived as something other than it is, namely, as an object of thought. But freedom is never *in abstracto.* If one would grant freedom an instant to make a choice between good and evil, without being in itself in either of the two positions, then precisely at that instant freedom is not freedom but a meaningless reflection.[17]

Freedom is not quite what is ordinarily understood by the notion of freedom. For Kierkegaard, though using the same word, is proposing a modification in the concept it expresses. So, freedom is not a kind of faculty in a man, by which he keeps his distance from good and evil and considers them. Good is freedom itself which consists of man's opening up of himself by relinquishing the finite. On the other hand, evil is nonfreedom, or the closing up of a man, which consists of not rejecting the immediate. In speaking of the demoniacal man, Kierkegaard writes:

> The demoniacal is the shut-up (Indesluttede), the demoniacal is dread of the good. . . . "Revelation" (Aabenbarelse) in this context is the good, for revelation is the first utterance of salvation.[18]

> The good of course signifies . . . the reintegration of freedom, redemption, salvation, or whatever name one would give it.[19]

The demoniacal man, shuts himself in, closes down his life and does not reject the immediate. This is evil according to Kierkegaard, since the good is the openness of imma-

nence that reveals itself. This openness characterizes the reflective consciousness of the ethical stage, and it is in fact the perpetual and articulated unfolding of the movement of becoming.

Now that Kierkegaard's reflections on the ethical stage have been presented and analyzed, the chief difference between it and the religious stage can be shown and properly described.

In the ethical stage, the problem still resides in the immanence of man; the question of the relationship between immanence and transcendence can not yet arise. The ethicist is well aware of the two dimensions of his consciousness, but his real ego, his "germinal sprout," his own transcendent existence, is still hidden from him. The *Postscript* includes a chapter entitled "A Glance at a Contemporary Effort in Danish Literature," in which Kierkegaard comments on his own previously published literary works. In dealing with *Either/Or*, Kierkegaard writes:

> The ethicist in *Either/Or* had saved himself through despair, abolishing concealment in self-relevation; but here was in my opinion a difficulty. . . . The difficulty is, that the ethical self is supposed to be found immanently in the despair, so that the individual by persisting in his despair at last wins himself. He has indeed used a determination of freedom: to choose himself, which seems to lessen the difficulty, a difficulty which presumably has not attracted the attention of many, since it is possible *philosophice* to doubt everything in a trice, and so to find the true beginning. But this avails nothing. When I despair, I use myself to despair, and therefore I can indeed by myself despair of everything; but when I do this, *I cannot by myself come back* [my italics]. In this moment

of decision it is that the individual needs divine assistance. . . .[20]

Despair, repentance or resignation are like facets of movement of negation, characteristic of the reflective consciousness. This movement does not pass beyond the limits of reflective consciousness, and the latter does not enclose the "being as being," which is man's real ego, or his ego as a positive determinant. Human immanence has only negative determinants, since each element in it is expressed through its negation. The ethical stage belongs to the phenomenal domain—the domain of the possible—and the passage from this domain to transcendent existence can only be carried out with "divine assistance." Faith alone can lead man back to his real ego, to his being as a postive determinant, and Kierkegaard uses and analyzes the story of Abraham in order to clarify his ideas in this connection.

According to the Genesis account, God puts Abraham to the test by asking him to sacrifice his only son. Abraham does not hesitate. He rises, saddles the donkeys, leaves his home, and heads for Mount Moriah to sacrifice his son, Isaac.

The story of Abraham is exploited in *Fear and Trembling* by one Johannes de Silentio, another pseudonymous author, this one a nonbeliever. He is able only to describe Abraham's behavior for us, without ascribing to it religious aspect. Abraham, Johannes de Silentio tells us, carried out two movements *simultaneously*. He relinquished the existence of Isaac, while believing "by virtue of the absurd" that God would not demand this sacrifice of him. On the one hand we have the movement of resignation, and on the other, repetition; Abraham, the knight of faith, gives up the existence of Isaac while protecting it by virtue of the absurd.

43

Now the first movement, that of resignation, involves only immanental factors, present in every human consciousness. Hence, every individual is capable of resigning himself:

> For the act of resignation faith is not required, for what I gain by resignation is my eternal consciousness, and this is a purely philosophical movement which I dare say I am able to make if it is required, and which I can train myself to make, for whenever any finiteness would get the mastery over me, I starve myself until I can make the movement. . . .[21]

Note how Kierkegaard often varies his terminology while expressing the same idea. Resignation, he tells us, is "a purely philosophical movement," that is, a movement which is carried out in immanence, and which anyone can make. In *Either/Or*, a comparable movement is called "repentance" or "despair," and is considered a reflection that is an action. But this movement, which is the movement of becoming, does not attain particular and transcendent existence; it is restricted to negating the finite phenomenon, or the finite as the possible. On the other hand, the real finite, the finite as positive determinant, is attained only through faith. The particular existence of Isaac is an example of this, and it is by means of the religious "leap" that Abraham attains faith.

> For the movements of faith must constantly be made by virtue of the absurd, yet in such a way, be it observed, that one does not lose the finite but gains it every inch. . . . I can describe the movements of faith . . . but I make other movements, I make the movements of infinity, whereas faith does the opposite: after having made the movements of infinity, it makes those of finiteness.[22]

44

The transition from the phenomenon to existence, from the possible to the real, is logically considered an absurdity. The transition from the possible to the real is, therefore, another kind of transition altogether. Nevertheless, Abraham is capable of making it, for he is a believer. Simultaneously he makes two opposing movements: the movement of resignation and the movement of repetition. He renounces Isaac's life, and at the same time by virtue of this absurdity he attains real faithful existence. But the believer "does not lose" the finite world (the finite as actual reality); on the contrary he achieves it through faith. The story of the sacrifice of Isaac is also a symbolic representation of human consciousness which discovers its transcendent dimension in faith. Since the ethicist is not yet a believer, he is aware of only the two immanent dimensions of his consciousness—the finite and the infinite. Johannes de Silentio makes only the movement of resignation (the movement of the infinite) and not that of repetition. The following picture is another symbolic representation of a believer's consciousness.

Johannes de Silentio compares the knight of resignation (or the knight of the infinite) and the knight of faith to two dancers:

> It is supposed to be the most difficult task for a dancer to leap into a definite posture in such a way that there is not a second when he is grasping after the posture, but by the leap itself he stands fixed in that posture. Perhaps no dancer can do it—that is what this knight [i.e., the knight of faith] does. . . . The knights of infinity are dancers and possess elevation. They make the movements upward, and fall down again. . . . But whenever they fall down they are not able at once to assume the posture, they vacillate an instant, and this vacillation shows that after all they are strangers in the world.[23]

45

The knight of the faith is an accomplished dancer. He can leap in such a way that he attains his position the very second he leaps. During the leap itself he is already set in his position. One can easily construe the "position" to be the symbol of transcendent existence. By virtue of the absurd, the knight of faith attains this existence by actually detaching himself from the phenomenal world and this detachment, which is resignation, is symbolized by the dancer's leap. What is inexplicable and absurd is the simultaneity of detachment and attachment, of negativity and positivity. The knight of faith does not lose his balance while leaping, because in doing so he does not relax his hold on transcendent reality; he is a believer. On the other hand, the knight of infinity, who represents only immanence, is a dancer who "vacillates" (vakle) for a moment, and this vacillation shows that he is a "stranger" (Fremmed) in the world. The ethicist is a stranger in the world because his world is still the world of possibles. Only the believer is firmly rooted in reality since he attains transcendent existence by the movement of repetition.

> Repetition is too transcendent for me also. I can circumnavigate myself, but I cannot erect myself above myself, I cannot find the Archimedean point." Thus says Constantius in *Repetition*.[24]

Johannes de Silentio says the same thing in *Fear and Trembling:*

> So this movement [of faith] I am unable to make. As soon as I would begin to make it everything turns around dizzily, and I flee back to the pain of resignation. I can swim in existence, but for this mystical soaring I am too heavy. To exist in such a way that my opposition to existence is

expressed as the most beautiful and assured harmony with it, is something I cannot do.[25]

Neither Johannes de Silentio nor Constantine Constantius is a believer. Both of them mention the difficulty of passing from the phenomenon, which is a negation ("an opposition to existence"), to transcendent existence (i.e., "being" as a positive determinant), which can be attained only in the religious stage.

Let us recapitulate our observations on the ethical stage of life. The transition from the esthetic to the ethical stage consists of the awakening of consciousness, which then becomes reflective. Man frees himself from the abstractions of the esthetic stage by reflection. The ethicist is aware of the finite as such, and does not consider it a foreign element, but rather as an essential determinant of his own consciousness. The emergence of each finite in him is constantly incorporated into the totality of consciousness which imparts an ever growing meaning. This is what the historic nature of ethical consciousness consists of. The ethicist attaches himself to his social environment and to his past history. He is "a universal man," in other words, simultaneously himself and humanity. This is not a matter of an abstract identification of the individual with humanity, but of a process of "becoming" during which the individual attempts to realize humanity in himself. And, this process has no finished and accomplished result, since the totality of consciousness, by always incorporating the newly discovered finite world, can never be realized in a single context.

In the ethical stage, one is aware only of the finite as possible, and not of the finite as real. The latter, which is a positive determinant, is attainable only through faith. Kierkegaard calls it "ulterior immediacy," by which he means

that it is not a primitive "given," but it is secondary, an immediacy after reflection. "For faith is not the first immediacy but a subsequent immediacy. The first immediacy is the esthetical. . . ."[26]

The three stages, so well known in Kierkegaard's pages, constitute therefore three steps in the gradual awakening of consciousness. The first is the step of esthetic immediacy, which is the positive immediacy and "givenness" of phenomena. But this positivity is only apparent, for the phenomenon is not actual reality but only a possibility to the thinking man. During the ethical stage, the apparent positivity of esthetical immediacy is dissipated. Then negativity appears in consciousness, which becomes reflective and aware of itself. During the religious stage, consciousness attains "subsequent immediacy," when the finite is grounded in transcendent existence.

4.

The Religious Consciousness

WHILE the esthetic and ethical stages express only the immanent and indwelling components of man, the religious stage explores the relationships between those immanent factors and those which are independent of and transcendent to a man. It is in this stage that man becomes "spirit," which is, as Kierkegaard says, "a relationship which relates itself to its own self, and in relating itself to its own self, relates itself to Another." This "other" is transcendent existence, i.e., the third dimension of human consciousness, and in fact its actual origin. In the *Postscript*, Kierkegaard makes a distinction between two sorts of "religiousness," which he calls religiousness A and religiousness B. The first type is the deepening of man's ethical attitude, the intensification of the movement of repentance which heightens the negativity of consciousness. But this religiousness is not Christianity, and can exist even in paganism.[1] For the A type of religiousness is only an expression of man's immanent behavior; it does not take into account the relationship between immanence and transcendence. Only Christianity —the B type of religiousness—is the expression of this relationship, which relation is constituted in a man in the moment of faith.

In speaking of the difference between religiousness A and religiousness B, Kierkegaard terms the first "pathetic" and the second "dialectical" and explains:

49

The distinction between the pathetic and the dialectical must, however, be more closely defined; for religiousness A is by no means undialectic, but it is not paradoxically dialectic. Religiousness A is the dialectic of inward transformation; it is the relation to an eternal happiness which is not conditioned by [a *something*] (et Noget) [my italics] but is the dialectic inward appropriation of the relationship, and so is conditioned only by the inwardness of the appropriation and its dialectic. Religiousness B, as henceforth it is to be called, or the paradoxical religiousness, as it has hitherto been called, or the religiousness which has the dialectical in [another place] (paa andet Sted), does on the contrary posit conditions, of such a sort that they are not merely deeper dialectical apprehensions of inwardness, but are a *definite something* [my italics] which defines more closely the eternal happiness. . . .[2]

The terms, "pathetic" and "dialectical" are used somewhat strangely here and ought to be briefly explained. Loosely speaking, Kierkegaard uses "pathetic" to refer to passions, feelings, impulses, sentiments, and emotions. Religiousness A is, thus, more like an extension and development of factors of pathos that are already present in human personality. This religiosity is not heightened and augmented by a strenuous "dialectical" factor now introduced from the outside. By "dialectical" here is meant principally a conceptual and intellective set of factors. Religiousness B introduces Jesus Christ, God in human flesh; and this new factor, from the outside, brings a sharper set of oppositions, a new context of self-definition, within which the pathos of the individual is more sharply augmented and focussed. In the latter, new concepts are forced to one's attention,

whereby one's pathos is deepened and considerably enriched.

The dialectic of "inward transformation" which the quoted passage deals with is in effect the process of becoming, and religiousness A expresses no more than this process. Kierkegaard says that this process is not consciously conditioned by a "definite something," which is transcendent existence. In fact, the dialectical tension of immanence is certainly conditioned by transcendent existence, since without the intrusive action of existence which gives birth to the phenomenon, immanence could not even exist. But so long as one considers only immanence, or rather so long as one does not have faith and remains circumscribed by immanental factors, one does not know that a transcendent being exists; and one can describe the dialectic of inwardness without taking this being into account. However, the moment one wishes to deal with individual existence, with that "something," one must go beyond immanence toward the dialectic of that altogether different sphere. In attaining this "something" through faith, man becomes spirit, and it is at this moment that he realizes that he is a sinner:

Sin-consciousness. This consciousness is the expression for the paradoxical transformation of existence. Sin is the new existence-medium. Apart from this, to exist (at existere) means merely that the individual having come into the world is present and is in the process of becoming; now it means that having come into the world he has become a sinner; apart from this, "to exist" is not a more sharply defining predicate, but is merely the form of all the more sharply defining predicates: one does not become anything in particular by coming into being, but

now, to come into being is to become a sinner. In the totality of guilt-consciousness, existence asserts itself as strongly as it can within immanence; but sin-consciousness is the breach with immanence. . . .[3]

When talking of immanence, the term "existence" designates consciousness itself, which is the synthesis of the particular and the general, or of the finite and the infinite. In immanence, "to exist" is not a predicate that adds any quality whatsoever to the phenomenon itself; here David Hume comes to mind. In *Postscript*, Kierkegaard often uses the terms "exist" (existere), "be" (være til), and "existing individual," and these terms denote man's immanent existence. The passage just quoted shows clearly that "exist" means simply "being what one is." The entire content of consciousness *is*. Logic, for instance, *is*; it has the immanent reality which every concept possesses. In discussing it, Kierkegaard says, in *The Concept of Dread*: "In logic no movement can *come about*, for logic *is*, and everything logical simply is. . . ."[4]

What Kierkegaard calls "guilt-consciousness" is, as we shall see later, again the intensification of the negativity of consciousness, which takes place in religiousness A. But in this religiousness we do not yet confront the question of the "breach" or the chasm separating immanent existence (that is, immanence itself as a synthesis of the finite and the infinite) from real existence which is transcendent and particular being. Only in "sin-consciousness" does man come to realize this breach. In order to see more clearly what Kierkegaard means by the category of "sin," let us review more carefully his observations on transcendent and particular existence.

In a discourse entitled "The Unchangeableness of God," published in 1855, Kierkegaard writes:

God is unchangeable. In His omnipotence He created this visible world—and made Himself invisible. He clothed Himself in the visible world as in a garment; He changes it as one who shifts a garment—Himself unchanged. Thus in the world of sensible things. In the world of events He is present everywhere in every moment; in a truer sense than we can say of the most watchful human justice that it is present everywhere, God is omnipresent, though never seen by any mortal; present everywhere in the least even as well as in the greatest. . . . In each moment every actuality is a possibility in His almighty hand; He holds all in readiness, in every instant prepared to change everything; the opinions of men, their judgements, human greatness and human abasement; He changes all, Himself unchanged. When everything seems stable (for it is only in appearance that the external world is for a time unchanged, in reality it is always in flux) and in the overturn of all things, He remains equally unchanged. . . .[5]

The world of phenomena is a continual creation of God. But the world of which man is conscious comprises only possibles; it does not encompass being *qua* being. In the *Journals*, Kierkegaard writes:

The confusion in the whole doctrine of "essence" in logic arises because one has not taken note of the fact that one operates always with the "concept" of existence. But this *concept* of existence is an ideality, and the difficulty is precisely in knowing whether existence enters into the concept. If it does, Spinoza may be right: *essentia involvit existentiam*, i.e., conceptual existence, or in other words, ideal existence. But on the other hand Kant is right in saying "that existence does not add any new determination of content to the concept." Obviously Kant honestly

thinks of existence, that is, empirical existence, as something that does not enter into concept. Everywhere in this plane of ideality, the principle is that *essentia* is *existentia* —if it is at all legitimate to use the concept of existence here. . . . But existence corresponds to particular reality; the individual, as Aristotle teaches it, remains outside or at least does not enter into the concept. For an individual animal, vegetable, or human being, existence (to be or not to be) is something very decisive; individual man does not, so far as I know, have an existence like that of the concept. . . .[6]

Transcendent, real, and individual existence is created by God or rather is itself God as manifested in nature. This existence intrudes upon consciousness at every moment, thus giving rise to the phenomena. But it "intrudes" consciousness while also retreating: it gives rise to the phenomenon and it withdraws at the same time. Let us look at the following passage from the *Journals*:

The whole question of the omnipotence of God and the relationship of his goodness to evil (instead of the distinction that God effects the good but allows the evil) can perhaps be solved simply thus: the *summum* of good that can be done to a being, and which raises him above anything that you can do to him, is to make him free. Omnipotence demands precisely this. This is what seems strange, since omnipotence should make him dependent. But if one wishes to think carefully about omnipotence, one will see that it must actually imply also the faculty of being able to withdraw, so that thereby a creature can be independent. . . . Every finite power makes a person dependent, only omnipotence can lead to independence, it alone can produce out of nothing what has subsistence,

as omnipotence never stops taking itself back. . . . The incomprehensible thing here is that not only is omnipotence capable of producing the most imposing thing of all: the visible totality of the universe, but also of producing the frailest of all: a being independent of it.[7]

It is the thrusting action of transcendent existence that makes the phenomena (visible totality) emerge. Omnipotence implies, Kierkegaard tells us, "also the faculty of being able to withdraw. . . . omnipotence never stops resurging." God manifests Himself in the world at every moment, and this world appears to us as a flux of phenomena which are differentiated qualitatively, thus constituting the visible totality of the universe. One does not see transcendent existence; one believes in it. Referring to the Cartesian principle of "cogito ergo sum," Kierkegaard in *The Sickness unto Death* formulates a principle of his philosophy: "To believe is to be."[8] The belief in God brings a man to his own real and actual existence. ". . . The real self," Kierkegaard tells us in *The Concept of Dread*, "is first posited by the qualitative leap."[9] The religious leap transfers man from immanence—the domain of possibles—to being *qua* being which is qualitatively different, that is, actual existence and not a possible. The adventure is, then, one of the features of human consciousness.

The passage we have just quoted deals with the question of good and evil in relation to freedom. Freedom, as we have seen, is both the choice and capacity to surrender. Man is free to say no to the finite which emerges at every moment, and this sets him free to absorb other finites which God will manifest to him. It is up to man to choose between good and evil, and the choice is actually made between freedom and nonfreedom, or between the opening or clos-

ing of consciousness. God wishes to set man free, for God wills good. Evil is produced by the human attitude which seeks to set itself up against God and consequently does not choose surrender or resignation. In this case consciousness egoistically attaches itself to the finite, which hides from it the transcendent existence that is its very origin. So long as man does not renounce the emerging finite, he cannot attain transcendent existence. In speaking of Abraham, Kierkegaard says in *Fear and Trembling*: ". . . Only he who draws the knife gets Isaac."[10]

Note that in drawing the knife, one raises the hand while withdrawing it slightly. This action represents the act of negation of consciousness, or the act of resignation which takes hold of the emerging phenomenon while recoiling. Transcendent existence is hidden behind every phenomenon, which is its veil, and only by removing the veil, that is, by negating the phenomenon, can man manage the "religious leap." Abraham received the existence of Isaac because he was ready to sacrifice him. Faith is *conditioned* by the prior attitude of resignation. Johannes de Silentio says: "The infinite resignation is the last stage prior to faith, so that one who has not made this movement has not faith. . . ."[11]

In *Postscript*, Kierkegaard emphasizes that religiousness B, that is, Christianity, is made possible by religiousness A, which expresses man's complete resignation from the finite world.[12] One cannot become a Christian without first renouncing the finite world. Repetition, the return to being *qua* being, will follow (and it could never precede) resignation. It is the negation of the finite which makes possible the faith in which man comes out of himself and attains transcendence. It follows that in the moment of faith (religiousness B) the believer achieves a double coming-out-of-him-

self at one time. The particular phenomenon is annihilated in him, and his consciousness thereby becomes available and free to incorporate still another phenomenon. Furthermore, the same negation of the phenomenon makes possible the religious leap toward transcendence. The coming-out-of-himself that the believer carries out is thus directed simultaneously toward transcendent existence and toward the finite phenomena that God is constantly manifesting. The believer's consciousness is completely open and completely free to receive the manifestations of God. This consciousness is the good. Evil, on the contrary, is a closure and narrowing in upon oneself, of which, as we have seen, the immanence of the demoniacal is an example.

But in coming out of oneself and attaining transcendent existence in the moment of faith, man realizes that he is a sinner. The category of "sin" that Kierkegaard posits has both a dialectical and a conceptual force, for it marks at one and the same time man's particular existence and actual personality, on the one hand, and on the other hand, the qualities of that personality, his fall, and his withdrawal from this existence. Let us consider the following passage:

> . . . Christianity . . . begins with the doctrine of sin. The category of sin is the category of the individual. Speculatively sin cannot be thought at all. The individual man is subsumed under the concept; one cannot think an individual man but only the concept man. . . . But as one cannot think an individual man, so neither can one think an individual sinner; one can think sin (the it becomes negative), but not an individual sinner. Just for this reason, however, there can be no seriousness about sin when it is merely thought. For seriousness is precisely the fact that thou and I are sinners. Seriousness is not sin in gen-

eral, but the emphasis of seriousness falls upon the sinner who is an individual.[13]

The category of sin, Kierkegaard tells us, is the category for the individual. Sin is not just thought about, it frames a man's particular existence; his self has sin as a positive determinant, which is hidden behind the phenomenal domain of consciousness. But the category of sin also expresses the fall of man. It is precisely in attaining transcendent existence that the believer fully comprehends the abyss, which separates the phenomenon from this existence. In fact, only the believer can realize this abyss. In the exaltation of the moment of faith, he looks down and then experiences anew the fall of man in the phenomenal domain of the finite. It is not thought which discovers this "breach" between immanence and transcendence, and man cannot think of sin because consciousness cannot attain existence rationally. Kierkegaard emphasizes that sin is a transcendent category and that no immanent activity, whether it be ethical science or psychology, can reveal sin or explain it:

> Every science has its province either in immanent logic, or in an immanence within a transcendence which it cannot explain. Now sin is precisely that transcendence, that *discrimen rerum*, by which sin enters into the individual as an individual.[14]

The emergence of each finite is itself the fall of man, for the finite as phenomenon only accentuates the distance that separates man from God. And it is up to man to struggle every instance against the emerging finite, in order to be able to attain particular and transcendent existence through faith. Speaking of the believer, Kierkegaard says:

> The believer, who reposes in and has his strength in the

consistency of the good, has an infinite fear of even the least sin, for he stands to lose infinitely.[15]

The believer makes an effort to renounce each finite, for fear that it might be a veil that hides transcendent existence from him, and in so doing transforms himself into a sinner. In contrast to the demoniacal man, who has "the consistency of sin" or "the consistency of evil," the believer renounces the finite and throws himself open to a revivifying transcendence. Nonetheless, being a human being, the believer is almost drowned in the finite world, and the moments of exaltation that he experiences through faith can only remind him of the distance between him and God. Kierkegaard writes:

> Besides, I would like to state, as I have often done, that the relationship with God develops in a sense as follows: the more one lives with Him, the more remote one feels oneself from Him, as He is raised infinitely higher.[16]

The struggle against the finite never ends. Despite his efforts, the believer remains a sinner, and he can only hope for the forgiveness of his sins by God, basing this hope on that decisive historical fact, which is the appearance of God among men. Christianity, or religiousness B is, according to Kierkegaard, "an existential communication" and not a point of doctrine.[17] It will be clear from the observations of Kierkegaard on indirect communication that Jesus of Nazareth, in his view, has the task of bringing man back to the being *qua* being hidden behind the particular phenomenon. At every moment man has need of Jesus whose aim is to save him from sin, i.e., from the fall of man which is confirmed by each emergence of a phenomenon. God has become a man, an individual, in order to bring man back to the particular existence by means of which He is manifested

59

in nature every moment. But although the Incarnation is a paradox that thought cannot comprehend, Christian faith nevertheless depends on reason, albeit in a negative way. In order to become a believer, man must recognize the inability of reflective human consciousness to attain transcendence. This means that he must grasp more intensively the negativity of his consciousness. In the *Journals*, Kierkegaard writes:

> This is the just thesis of Saint-Victor (Helfferich: Die christlich Mystik, Vol. 1, p. 368).

> In matters that are beyond reasons, faith certainly is not actually supported by reason, for faith does not comprehend what it believes; but there is certainly here something through which reason is determined or decides to give faith its due although it is not capable of entirely comprehending faith.

> This is what I developed in *Postscript.* . . . The activity of reason is precisely to understand that it [the paradox] cannot and need not be understood. This is a negative category, but it is as dialectical as any positive category. . . . Now, in the face of the paradox, one's bulwark is faith. It believes in the paradox; and now, to come back to the words of Huges de Saint-Victor, the means whereby reason can certainly be predetermined to give faith its due is by intensifying the negative categories of the paradox. In all, it is a fundamental error to deny that negative concepts exist; the highest principles of all thought or their proof are definitely negative. Human reason has limits; that is where the negative concepts are. Frontier actions are negative, they work backwards. . . .[18]

Although faith goes beyond any reason-giving, it nevertheless depends on a rational awareness of the limits of rea-

soning whereby reason can be mitigated. In *Philosophical Fragments*, Kierkegaard says that the supreme passion of reason is to seek a collision, i.e., it wishes to discover something that thought cannot think.[19] Human reason attains the summit of its power the very moment it recognizes its failure, its own negation, thus becoming involved in "frontier actions that are negative." And it is recognition of this failure which makes Christian faith possible. Religiousness B is conditioned, Kierkegaard tells us, by religiousness A, and the latter is simply the intensification of this kind of negativity in consciousness.

Before proceeding further, it might be well to summarize a bit the argument to this point. We have already seen Kierkegaard's differences between the pathetic and the dialectical. The former involves passions and feelings, and the latter more typically, concepts and appropriate oppositions between them. Consciousness, we have said, is being documented in Kierkegaard's pages, almost as a process of growth, from the esthetic stage, through the ethical, and into the religious A and B. What this involves is that the individual, gradually and in a variety of ways, develops those powers to make himself his own object. To be conscious is to have oneself as the direct object of wish, desire, thought, and feeling. Or, if one remembers the previous delineations, it is as if one begins with dreams, with vague and indefinite wishes, most of them quite rootless, simply to be suffered. Gradually, though, one really acquires a consciousness. But, Kierkegaard's point is precisely that this consciousness can not be acquired only by means of self-reflection. The sense of sin, whereby one senses in a deeply misgiving way, whereby one subsumes himself negatively as wrong before God, this sense of sin is a crisis in pathos which also forces a new dialectic, new concepts upon one. And it is of such stuff that consciousness is forged.

5.

Consciousness and Religions A and B

WE have seen that reflective consciousness characterizes the ethical stage of life. Religiousness A is actually
the intensification of this reflective stage of consciousness.
The believer in this religiousness is aware of each finite that
emerges in his consciousness, and realizes that the finite is
proof of nonrealization of the synthesis of his consciousness.
The believer of religiousness A can never realize this totality as he is constantly engaged in the process of becoming,
and thus always remains ahead of himself. Despite the impossibility of realizing this synthesis, however, he continues
to seek it, and this synthesis, in the religious stage, has several appellations. It is "the absolute telos," "the eternal happiness," "the absolute good," and finally, "God." Let us consider the following passage:

> The totality of guilt-consciousness is the most edifying
> factor in religiousness A. The edifying element in the
> sphere of religiousness A is essentially that of immanence,
> it is the annihilation by which the individual puts himself
> out of the way in order to find God, since precisely the in-
> dividual himself is the hindrance. Quite rightly the edify-
> ing is recognizable here also by the negative, by self-anni-
> hilation, which in itself finds the God-relationship, is
> based upon it, because God is the basis when every
> obstacle is cleared away, and first and foremost the indi-

vidual himself in his finiteness, in his obstinacy against God.[1]

By renouncing the finite, the believer of religiousness A finds the God-relationship in himself. But it should be noted in this connection that religiousness A treats God as a negative determinant and not as positive and real existence. The God of immanence may be found in any religion, even in paganism;[2] He is the expression of the religious feelings man acquires as soon as he comes to realize the finiteness of the human condition and opens himself toward what lies beyond it. Every act of resignation gives birth to the God of immanence, and this God is the totality of consciousness, the "all":

> . . . for in immanence God is neither a something (He being all and infinitely all), nor is He outside the individual, since edification consists precisely in the fact that He is in the individual.[3]

The God of immanence is the eternal happiness which the believer looks forward to when he renounces his finiteness. The relationship with this happiness obtains at every moment since the believer never ceases self-resignation. We have already said that the totality of consciousness expresses itself by the negation of the phenomenon; the annihilation of the finite is at the same time the self-confirmation of the totality of consciousness. Now this relationship appears in the religious stage as the "absolute relationship to the absolute telos" which is at the same time a "relative relationship to relative ends." The believer, Kierkegaard tells us, maintains ". . . simultaneously a relationship to the absolute *telos* and to relative ends. . . ."[4] It is the simultaneity of the two relationships that is important here. The

believer relates to the absolute telos, to the immanent God, while living in the finite world, and his relationship to God is based on the continual detachment from the finite:

> ... The individual who sustains an absolute relationship to the absolute *telos* may very well exist in relative ends, precisely in order to exercise the absolute relationship in renunciation.[5]

The believer makes an effort to attain eternal happiness which in principle is unattainable. This is therefore a task which is never accomplished, since the synthesis and wholeness of religious consciousness can never be realized. Here we touch the same point that we dealt with in the preceding chapter in describing the process of becoming in the ethical consciousness. The believer of religiousness A, as well as the ethical man, is conscious of the process of becoming, and he is continually trying to realize his own self. But as the synthesis of consciousness, the totally healed consciousness, can never be realized, the believer can actually give expression to this totality only by means of his own resignation, suffering, and guilt. Resignation, suffering, and guilt are intensifications of the movement of repentance that the ethical man takes part in, and they represent the necessary negations that must go on. In *Philosophical Fragments*, Kierkegaard writes:

> All coming into existence is a *suffering,* and the necessary cannot suffer; it cannot undergo the suffering of the actual, which is that the possible (not only the excluded possibility but also the accepted possibility) reveals itself as nothing (viser sig som Intet) in the moment it becomes actual, for the possible is [annihilated in the] (tilintetgjort) actual.[6]

64

In this passage, Kierkegaard uses the term "actual" to designate the immanent being, i.e., the mental reality of the finite which *is*. Now the possible, i.e., the phenomenon, appears as a negation from its birth. It is at once the admission of the negation of the healthy and totally synthesized consciousness and the negation of itself. In becoming actual, that is, in emerging, the possible is already annihilated, and the aspirations of the believer to eternal happiness are expressed in this annihilation. Kierkegaard notes religiousness of the A type to have its own pathetic quality, and the existential pathos of the believer culminates, he says, in the feeling of guilt. When man recognizes that he is the furthest away from eternal happiness, this happiness finds its inverse yet loftiest expression in the feeling of guilt. The believer makes passionate attempts to attain eternal happiness, without, of course, succeeding in accomplishing this task. The word passion, in Danish as well as other languages, connotes something of the same meaning as suffering. The consciousness of a man is thus that of a suffering and contrite passion.

In order to better understand the behaviour of the believer in religiousness A, let us consider the following passage:

In existence the individual is a concretion, time is concrete, and even while the individual deliberates he is ethically responsible for his use of time. Existence is not an abstract spurt but steady striving and a *continuous meanwhile* [my italics]; even at the instant when the task is clearly set there has been some waste, for meanwhile time has passed, and the beginning was not made at once. Thus things go backward: the task is presented to the individual in existence, and just as he is ready to cut at once a fine figure (which only can be done *in abstracto* and on

paper, because the loose trousers of the abstractor are very different from the strait jacket of the exister) and wants to begin, it is discovered that a new beginning is necessary, the beginning upon the immense detour of dying from immediacy, and just when the beginning is about to be made at this point, it is discovered that there, since time has meanwhile been passing, an ill beginning is made, and that the beginning must be made by becoming guilty and from that moment increasing the total capital guilt by a new guilt at a usurious rate of interest.[7]

The particular phenomenon is a constraint upon the realization of the homogeneous consciousness. The realization, or emergence, of a single possibility is also the loss of the others, since one thus necessarily renounces "what one could have become." But it is precisely in this loss that that homogeneous and seamless consciousness as such is betokened in all its power and demands its realization on the part of man. At each step the man takes, it contemplates him and says reproachfully: "Is that all you can do?" Compared with the full range of possibilities, with the scope of our competence, the single possibility is, when it emerges, an "ill beginning." And then one must begin with another step, since each step is not progress, but, on the contrary, failure or retreat. Thus one advances by drawing backwards, for it is precisely in comprehending one's failure that one soars to get free of it. Eternal happiness shows itself through guilt. So with the complexities of human consciousness. Guilt is the appeal of eternal happiness which pushes man toward a new beginning. But it is clear that the immanent powers of the believer thus set a task which is never accomplished, since each beginning almost seems a setback. Each beginning shows "that a new beginning is

necessary, the beginning upon the immense detour of dying from immediacy."

As an event, a particular episode occupies only a temporal moment. But this moment is by no means an isolated atom of time; it is a "continuous meanwhile." For temporal moments also have to be brought together. Just as the isolated phenomenon acquires meaning from consciousness that makes it an object within which it rests, so the temporal moment lives in a generality of time. The loss of the homogeneousness of consciousness produced by the emergence of each finite thing occasions an awareness of time gone by. At each moment in life, one has already lost what one could have become; one's youth departs as a multitude of possibilities that might have been. The constraint upon realizing the perfected consciousness awakens in us nostalgia for the youth that no longer exists, that is the past. One becomes old at each moment, at each emergence of a particular event. On the other hand, the awareness of a loss is also a thrust toward the activity which should make up the delay or lack. Time gone by makes us strive for our salvation, for the eternal happiness that awaits us and is both the incentive and the end of our activity. Eternity looms up as the future.[8] The three dimensions of time are thus condensed in each current moment, which is a "continuous meanwhile." We shall consider the point more carefully in the last chapter of this book.

The life of the believer of religiousness A is thus a continual effort in search of perfection. The eternal happiness that he expects is no one particular thing;[9] it is, rather, an infinite horizon of becoming, which opens up before him as a result of his renunciation of what he already is. The believer lives in the immediacy while simultaneously renouncing it, for he recognizes its insufficiency and finiteness. The

67

emergence of the finite only hinders the unveiling of the other phenomena, and each particular encounter with the world is but the very veil which hides the totality of the world. When it is a question of the ethical and religious stages in which the particular phenomenon becomes "a choice," the same considerations recur. Any single and present choice is a constraint that demonstrates man's ethical imperfection, since that choice can never be a complete fulfillment of everything he could have been. Now it is precisely by renouncing the finite that the believer attempts to improve constantly, and it is through an awareness of his guilt that he glimpses eternal happiness. Again, it is not thought alone but also the chastened pathos, a contrite spirit, which helps him. But the ever-present impossibility of achieving this happiness only increases the believer's feeling of guilt, and it is in assuming this guilt more and more deeply that the believer of religiousness A prepares for the religious leap toward transcendence by which he will become a Christian.

However, the religious feeling that characterizes religiousness A does not necessarily lead man to Christianity. Kierkegaard develops and clarifies his ideas on Christianity in about eighty discourses, primarily in *Works of Love* and in *Training in Christianity*. These works clearly demonstrate that we have here an ideal of an extremely rigorous sort. Kierkegaard himself was not sure that he was a real Christian; and when he wrote *Training in Christianity*, he was very clear that his own behavior did not exemplify the Christian ideal which the work presents. The road to Christianity is full of obstacles, and the danger of diverging menaces man at every moment. Humor offers an example of such a detour. Kierkegaard's reflections on humor and irony constitute, in our opinion, the most important part of

his philosophy, and only by studying them can one understand Kierkegaard's philosophy and his ideas on Christianity. We shall take up the theme of humor again when we discuss Kierkegaard's theory of communication, and we shall limit ourselves here to presenting humor as a detour which takes man away from the religious life.

Again, though, it is well to remember that Kierkegaard is very intent upon plotting the enormous variety of ways that human consciousness develops. Even when approaching the most strenuous reaches of Christian consciousness, Kierkegaard finds it necessary to show his reader that humor and irony are also forms of consciousness. Ordinarily we speak of a "sense of humor" and "an attitude of irony." But Kierkegaard's interest is to show that when humor has as its object the whole of the world and even man's fate, then it has some resemblance to a religious consciousness. So, too, with irony, but for different reasons as we shall subsequently note. The point to remark here is simply that even such behavioral features as humor and irony are included in the panoply of human consciousness. Kierkegaard is a most unusual philosopher for having charted their characteristics in such a context.

In *Postscript*, Kierkegaard considers humor to be "the border line for the religiousness of hidden inwardness," i.e., of religiousness A. Like the believer, the man of humor is well aware of the relativity and precariousness of the human condition, and he assumes responsibility for this and feels guilty. But instead of awaiting eternal happiness, he withdraws at the last moment and the inner tension he feels is resolved in jest. While the renunciation of the finite leaves the believer open to the future and the possible realization of eternal happiness, the humorist, who likewise is finite, does not relate to this happiness.[10] He renounces the world

because it appears as an enigma which he cannot decipher and which sometimes even seems to lack sense. But instead of persevering in a search which might discern some sense or other, instead of intensifying guilt feelings, the humorist makes fun of all of it and thus escapes into jest.

Now let a humorist express himself, and he will speak for example as follows: "What is the meaning of life? Aye, tell me that; how should I know, we are born yesterday and know nothing. But one thing I do know, namely, that it is most comfortable to stride unknown through the world, without being known to His Majesty the King, Her Majesty the Queen, Her Majesty the Queen Mother, His Royal Highness, Prince Ferdinand; for such aristocratic acquaintanceships only make life troublesome and painful, just as it must be troublesome for a prince who lives in straitened circumstances in a country town to be recognized by his royal family."[11]

Instead of facing squarely the problems posed by life, the humorist, though fully conscious of the problems, makes a digression and seeks a joke. But it must be noted that the humorist does not negate the religious sentiment which is hidden in his joke, though he has actually revoked it. In *Postscript*, Kierkegaard emphasizes the fact that humor combines pain and pleasure. Beneath the laugh or smile of the humorist, we discern the suffering of a mature soul who knows the precarious and ephemeral character of human life. The humorist, who is certainly a subjective thinker, has a potential which is as tragic as it is comic. Within each man are the factors, the finite and the infinite; but the humorist seeks within their contrasts that which gives rise to a jest, and thereby the contrast itself is toned down and blurred. Through the joke, he rises above the human condition

whose futility is accentuated by this very superiority. The humorist recognizes his constraint at the same time as he gets free of it.

But humor is, as we have seen, a detour which diverts man from the religious life. All religious life is characterized by resignation, by which man keeps his distance. As soon as one accentuates the given factors, as soon as one latches on to them in a positive fashion, one is no longer a believer. Now the jesting of the humorist is a regression as compared to the attitude of the believer in religiousness of the A type. While the latter tirelessly resigns himself, the humorist retreats back upon himself and latches on to his capacities to keep smiling at the last moment. Jesting produces complacency which the humorist finds comfortable, and he is complacent about himself. Although he renounces the world as things impinge upon him, still he cherishes whatever can be made compliant by his joking.

When one uses laughter and the jest as a way to take oneself and the world, one is no longer a believer, neither of religiousness A nor of religiousness B. The man of humor, Kierkegaard tells us, apprehends suffering in intimate connection with existence, but revokes its essential significance for the existing individual.[12] In attaching himself to his capacities at the last moment, the humorist makes impossible the coming-out-of-oneself which leads man to transcendence, and which is conditioned upon the intensification of the movement of resignation. The whole value of belief depends on this movement of passion, and only in renouncing immanental capacities absolutely can a man become a Christian. Now it is in Christianity that the perfect resignation is attained. In religiousness B, the believer, or rather the Christian, heightens resignation and transforms it into a *love* which is total self-abnegation. In Christian

love, there remains no trace of self-satisfaction or self-complacency.[13] Let us now consider Kierkegaard's observation on this love.

While religiousness A realizes no more than the inward capacities of every man, religiousness B, which is Christianity, simultaneously realizes these, as well as achieving something that is transcendent and not within ordinary limits. Christianity considers man to be a spirit, and during his lifetime the Christian puts together several factors which would otherwise be discrepant and divisive. On the one hand there are the finite limits, the raw material of the physical and mental life. Then there are the drives and wishes that push him to goals and aspirations that are the infinite. But lastly, there is that transcendent existence which is revealed when he is face to face with Jesus. To put these together is to become a spirit. Now man *qua* spirit *is* love. The Christian love described by Kierkegaard is not a romantic feeling or dream. It is a new form of human consciousness constituted and made by its own origin in transcendent existence. Love is a new ingredient. One learns from Jesus to love the world and men as God loved them.

Like Christ, the model, the Christian is all love. This love has a transcendent origin from which it emanates constantly. In *Works of Love,* Kierkegaard points out that man cannot "know" the origin of this love rationally; he believes in it.[14] Christian love is created in the moment of faith during which the relationship between immanence and transcendence is established, and this relationship is expressed in God's commandment: "You shall love your neighbor as yourself." This commandment actually reflects the three dimensions of human consciousness. For one must love transitively. Love is not only a feeling; it is a kind of consciousness.

We have seen that in the reflective consciousness the phenomenon is confirmed by its own negation. It affirms its particular nature precisely while relinquishing its place to consciousness in general. Now when consciousness becomes loving, the finite and ordinary desires appear to it as egoisms which need to be annihilated. Thus love requires and subsumes self-abnegation. In *Philosophical Fragments,* Kierkegaard writes:

> Self-love lies as the ground of love; but the paradoxical passion of self-love when at its highest pitch wills precisely its own downfall. This is also what love desires, so that these two are linked in mutual understanding in the passion of the moment, and this passion is love. . . . self-love is indeed submerged but not annihilated; it is taken captive and becomes love's *spolia opima,* but may again come to life, and this is love's temptation.[15]

In *Works of Love,* Kierkegaard tells us that Christianity presupposes that man loves himself, and in bidding him to love his neighbor, adds only "as yourself."[16] In Christianity, on the one hand there is both an affirmation of man's self-love, and on the other hand also its negation. It is therefore clear that the commandment "You shall love your neighbor as yourself" is loosely analogous to the features of the phenomenon in the reflective consciousness. The ordinary phenomenon there affirms itself by negating itself, and in the same way self-love is accentuated in Christianity while being vanquished and transforming itself into love of another. This, according to Kierkegaard, is also where we find the temptations of love. We have already seen that in a single kind of cognitive consciousness, the phenomenon requires "a choice of surrender" and that the Christian "is a man of will who no longer wants his will." These are the

characteristics that are always expressed by the dialectical behavior of the particular phenomenon. And it is precisely in the negation of this phenomenon, in its "surrender" before the totality of consciousness, that the other person is produced in consciousness. As we have seen, the other person is a possible which appears in consciousness as part of the general context. The category of "other" is thus an internal determinant of consciousness itself. Kierkegaard makes this point more clearly in *Works of Love*:

> *Who, then, is one's neighbor?* The word is clearly derived from *neahgebur* (near-dweller); consequently your neighbor is he who dwells nearer than anyone else, yet not in the sense of partiality, for to love him who through favoritism is nearer to you than all others is self-love—"Do not the heathens also do the same?" Your neighbor, then, is nearer to you than all others. But is he also nearer to you than you are to yourself? No, that he is not, but he is just as near or ought to be just as near to you as you are to yourself. The concept of *neighbor* really means a duplicating of one's own self. *Neighbor* is what philosophers would call the *other*, that by which the selfishness in self-love is to be tested. As far as thought is concerned the *neighbor* or *other* need not even exist. If a man living on a desert island formed his mind according to the command, he could by forsaking self-love be said to love his neighbor.[17]

It is in obeying the commandment "You shall love your neighbor as yourself" that man creates for himself the other as his own object. Love requires an object, the neighbor. Remember that the relationship between a man and the other is already established in the ethical stage during which man tries through repentance to realize "the univer-

sal man" in himself. Christian love is the intensification of this very relationship:

> There is in the whole world not a single person who can be recognized with such ease and certainty as one's neighbor. You can never confuse him with anyone else, for indeed all men are your neighbor.[18]

The other is always close to the believer, even if he is on "a desert island." Kierkegaard says also that the person who loves "never loses" the other. The other belongs to, and is sustained by, the very consciousness of the believer, and it is his self-abnegation which gives the other his birth and status to that believer.

In saying that the other is "all men," Kierkegaard does not mean that the other is an abstraction like the notion of "the public." Abstractions of this sort, which will be discussed in the next chapter, are not allowed the believer. For he is attentive to each emerging instance, but not to their collectivity. The negation of his particular wishes and desires does not push him toward an abstraction, but rather toward the particular individual; and thus his own consciousness becomes enriched, confirmed, and even healed. Similarly, in Christian love, one loves one's "neighbor," the nearest individual, but this means also that one loves all men in turn. Christian love also enlarges one's consciousness toward the diversity of men. In *Works of Love*, Kierkegaard repeatedly describes the Christian's sensitivity to this diversity and to the qualitative differences which the finite world reveals to us.[19] The Christian is familiar with all the peculiarities of his neighbor, and in loving him he also loves everybody.

The Christian love which Kierkegaard discusses thus supposes the attitude of resignation, accentuated to the highest

degree and transformed into a total abnegation of self. The Christian renounces the finite and immediate world entirely, and he thus keeps his distance from every worldly element. Kierkegaard continually accentuates the difference between Christian love and any other feeling of love or friendship in which calculations are involved. A love that depends on calculations only demonstrates man's attachment to the finite world. On the other hand, Christian love does not depend on any object, since it is nothing less than the fundamental attitude of the believer who renounces every finite object:

> Erotic love is determined by the object; friendship is determined by the object; only love to one's neighbor is determined by love. Since one's neighbor is every man, unconditionally every man, all distinctions are indeed removed from the object. Therefore genuine love is recognizable by this, that its object is without any of the more definite qualifications of difference, which means that this love is recognizable only by love.[20]

Christianity imposes love on the believer; it says that you *shall* love your neighbor. The Christian is constrained to love his neighbor by God's demand. Love is an absolute duty.[21] But Christianity, Kierkegaard tells us, imposes this duty only in order to make man free.[22] We have already seen that freedom is man's coming-out-of-himself, which leads him to the unveiling of phenomena and to transcendent existence. The free man is the one who relates to what is "other" than himself, and he does this through resignation. God wishes man to love and to renounce the immediate precisely so that he may be free. Christian love establishes the relationship between man and his neighbor, and it does so by introducing the other into the very capacities

and powers of man. Kierkegaard writes: *"If it were not a duty to love, then there would be no concept of neighbor at all."*[23]

In imposing self-abnegation upon man, Christianity transforms him into a social being who is free to welcome the other. If man does not renounce immediacy, if he identifies himself positively and egoistically with the contents of his immanence, he will become a being who is isolated and enclosed so that he is in danger of losing all articulation. The immanence of the estheticist is an example of this. On the other hand, the immanence of the Christian is a coming-out-of-himself, whereby his consciousness is directed toward "others" as well as toward the transcendent existence of which Jesus is the supreme example. It is by Christian love that man becomes a "spirit," since this love establishes the relationship between man, his neighbor, and God. The three dimensions of consciousness find complete expression in this relationship, and imply each other reciprocally. The following excerpts, one of which has already been quoted, demonstrate this relationship clearly:

... it is self-renunciation which discovers that God is.[24]

He towards whom I have a duty is my neighbor, and when I fulfill my duty I prove that I am a neighbor.[25]

There is in the whole world not a single person who can be recognized with such ease and certainty as one's neighbor. You can never confuse him with anyone else, for indeed all men are your neighbor.[26]

It is through self-renunciation that man projects and discovers the other in himself, and it is in loving the other that one's love of God is expressed. Self-renunciation provides the condition for the creation of the other in immanence on

77

the one hand, and contact with transcendence on the other.

Love is abiding, Kierkegaard tells us. The Christian continues to love as long as he lives, since his new power itself, now immanent to him, is love. His new immanence is a perpetual movement during which he exerts himself to accomplish his duty toward others. The love of others is a debt that constantly increases even while one attempts to pay it off. It is an infinite involvement; the more one loves the more one needs to love. The immanence of the Christian is "a task" to accomplish,[27] a movement in which each moment is an action, a work, not an idle occurrence:

> When it is a duty to be in the debt of love to each other, *this being in debt is not a fanatical expression, is not a fancy of love, but is action; therefore, with the help of duty, love continues Christianly in action, in the movement of action, and thereby in infinite debt.*[28]

Christian love puts the believer in debt to his neighbor, and this love also intensifies the guilt-consciousness that the believer of religiousness A experiences. It should be noted that in Danish, the word for guilt is "Skyld" and the word for debt is "Gjeld." Both words are of German origin, and Heidegger points out at least one etymological relationship between them. Kierkegaard's own observations on guilt and love likewise establish this relationship, the point being that we have here a human attitude that pushes man to transcend himself. According to Kierkegaard, however, man transcends himself toward a particular being, and this transcendence takes place only in Christian love. Guilt, on the other hand, concerns only immanence, in which one transcends toward the other as an immanent entity. Furthermore, in religiousness A, where guilt is emphasized, it is still possible to find an escape hatch like humor that stops man from renouncing himself entirely. Only in Christian love is

a relationship established with transcendence as well as with others, and it is the absolute character of Christian abnegation which makes this relationship possible.

In the work we are studying at present, Kierkegaard deals with "the works" of love. These works include an inclusive mercy, absolute self-abnegation, as well as religious hope. A work of love requires that very attitude of the believer which is self-renunciation. The fact that one remembers a dead person is also a work of love. Kierkegaard considers the love of the dead to be the purest love, and because of this purity, it is the criterion for all other love.[29] A pure love is one which does not depend on the response and which cannot be calculated. Any calculation is evidence of self-love. But one cannot profit from a dead man. He does not respond to our manifestations of concern, and he does not love us more or less because of them. He can no longer love, and in loving him *despite* his silence, one demonstrates the purest love. This love then is that kind of subjectivity which, while it has an object, does not depend on any object. Kierkegaard's remarks on love for the dead demonstrate once more that the other has to be taken into one's immanental contexts, and thereby it becomes a determinant of consciousness itself. The other is, in this sense, within oneself, even if he is dead, and even if one is on a desert island.

Having dealt with the religious stage of life, we shall now recapitulate and consider the three stages of life together.

In *Postscript*, after presenting religiousness A and religiousness B, Kierkegaard returns to reflections on the three stages of life. In the following passage, Kierkegaard sums up the differences between these stages:

All interpretations of existence rank in accordance with the degree of the individual's dialectical apprehension of

inwardness. . . . If the individual is in himself undialectical and has his dialectic outside himself, then we have the *aesthetic interpretation.* If the individual is dialectical in himself inwardly in self-assertion, hence in such a way that the ultimate basis is not dialectic in itself, inasmuch as the self which is at the basis is used to overcome and assert itself, then we have the *ethical interpretation.* If the individual is inwardly defined by self-annihilation before God, then we have *religiousness A.* If the individual is paradoxically dialectic, every vestige of original immanence being annihilated and all connection cut off, the individual being brought to the utmost verge of existence, then we have the *paradoxical religiousness.* This paradoxical inwardness is the greatest possible, for even the most paradoxical determinant, if after all it is within immanence, leaves as it were a possibility of escape, of a leaping away, of a retreat into the eternal behind it; it is as though everything had not been staked after all. But the breach makes the inwardness the greatest possible.[30]

The consciousness of the estheticist is not properly reflective, for he gets lost in abstractions that lack articulation. The consciousness of the estheticist "dissolves into nothing at all, into an atmosphere, into a single color." The finite as such is a strange element to him, an obstacle that comes from outside and prevents his romantic dreams from flowering. In the esthetic stage, the tension between the general and the particular becomes the contrast between man's romantic world and the ordinary daily circumstances of life. The estheticist thus has his dialectic "outside himself."

"If the individual is dialectical in himself . . . we have the ethical interpretation." The ethical stage, the stage of reflection, breaks one's immanental synthesis in twain. It divides one's consciousness and makes it dialectical in itself. There

is an internalization of the dialectical tension when the determinants become clear. The ethicist becomes more fully conscious by separating the finite and infinite which were otherwise a totality. The ethical man brings about a breach between "is" and "ought," between the state of affairs and the way they ought to be. This is a bifurcation and a breach in consciousness. One then feels guilt, for one then has realized a criterion by which to criticize and to construe oneself. One is no longer innocent and whole. One now suffers dread, anguish, fear, and guilt. As Kierkegaard says, the ethical man seeks "to assert himself." He believes he is capable of actually healing his own ego by winning out over this dialectical tension. But this is the very point that Kierkegaard rejects when he criticizes Judge William's ideas in *Postscript*. As we have seen, Kierkegaard insists that only "divine assistance" can guarantee the return of the self, that happy synthesis, which is involved in the movement of resignation and despair. But the factors one already has cannot do anything positive, since it is always the negative that is expressed and the breach that is widened in the dialectical interplay. The true ego of man, his self as positive and whole, comes to birth only in the religious leap.

In religiousness A the movement of resignation intensifies and becomes transformed into "a self-annihilation before God." Religious feeling is aroused when man recognizes the limit of everything human, and no longer seeks to mend himself by his own capacities. The believer of religiousness A is passionately interested in his existence. He constantly seeks himself in it, while he is nevertheless aware of the fact that no positive resolution can be found. In religiousness A reality, true existence, is not yet attained, but passionate interest in this reality prepares man for the religious leap through which he attains a transcendent existence and a new synthesis of the discrepant factors.

However, in religiousness A there is a "possibility of escape" with the help of humor. Like the believer in religiousness A, the humorist also renounces immediacy. But at the last moment the humorist catches hold of the contrarities and delights in them. Joking makes his own cleft in consciousness more palatable to him, and he stays there as long as he can, always putting off the religious leap.

"If the individual is paradoxically dialectic, every vestige of original immanence being annihilated . . . we have the paradoxical religiousness." The self-renunciation of the Christian is a complete coming-out-of-himself by which he is given a new and transcendental existence. He is no longer explicable by factors common to all. The individual then becomes a spirit which is "paradoxically dialectic." The triple relationship between the finite and infinite of immanence on the one hand, and between immanence and transcendence on the other, is established during the moment of faith.

It should be added that in speaking of religiousness A, Kierkegaard says: "Religiousness A . . . prevents the exister from becoming abstract in immanence. . . ."[31] The believer does not lend himself to abstraction since he takes the finite with a new seriousness. This sensitivity in regard to the finite appears in the ethical stage, and it is intensified in the religious stage to the point where the believer, in religiousness B, accepts the finite as actual existence. Kierkegaard adds: "But the breach makes the inwardness the greatest possible." It is precisely this contact with transcendent existence which broadens human immanence and gives it the highest degree of inwardness. The most profound immanence is the one which is the most sensitive to the emergence of the finite phenomena constantly manifested by God. On the other hand, an alienated immanence does not "receive" these manifestations at all.

6.

The Alienation of Consciousness

HUMAN consciousness does not encompass being *qua* being. Unless man makes the religious "leap," he remains forever far from God and enclosed in an immanence which never finds its ontological basis. The third dimension of consciousness, the transcendent dimension, is hidden from him, and in consequence the two immanent factors in consciousness (the finite and the infinite) often lose their distinctiveness. In such cases, consciousness as a whole becomes disfigured and deformed. It is then alienated by the loss of its negative trait, and it becomes wholly positive. This false stance, being positive without being negative, makes for the alienation of consciousness, as opposed to the healthy consciousness where the negativity is also ingredient. The latter is, for example, never a completed and positive fact, but always a movement of becoming in which what is not is becoming something. So is the fate of a human consciousness.

We have seen that the believer unceasingly puts himself into the movement of resignation, thus actually living the negative character of his consciousness. For to resign is to give up in order to become something else. The believer does not consider any present state to be his completed existence; it is for him rather another possibility, something to be overcome. In *Judge for Yourselves!*, Kierkegaard writes:

In Christianity everything goes by pairs (Fordoblelse),

or every determinant factor of Christianity is in the first instance its own opposite, whereas in the merely human or worldly sphere each is simply and directly what it is.[1]

In Christianity, to lose is to gain, humiliation is the means of new exaltation, and suffering or "dying from the finite" is the way to salvation. This dialectical quality of the determinants is anticipated even in the ethical stage of life. The self-realization of the ethicist takes form through the perpetual movement of repentance, and in religiousness A, eternal happiness is approached through feelings of guilt. The positive is always reinforced by the negative, and Christianity only accentuates this determinant. But in the "merely human or worldly sphere," i.e., where what is given is considered a domain separated from transcendence and God, everything is positive, everything is taken to be what it is. The more positive everything is understood to be, the more consciousness is alienated. Alienation appears when man considers the content of his present life to be his actual reality. In a nonalienated context, a "table," for example, is only a general sign designating a diversity of particular phenomena which manifest themselves ceaselessly. On the other hand, to an alienated consciousness, this abstract concept itself becomes the name for the real, being erroneously considered only for what it is. Similarly, the estheticist tends to substitute his dreams for reality, by attaching himself positively to the contents of his dream. He is more in love with love than with an actual woman, and his dream is only an abstract generality, or a mood (Stemning). It is related to nothing outside of itself. It is, thus, completely self-contained, immanent to itself and abstract.

But there are cases in which consciousness is alienated from its own nature not because it is lost in abstractions, but

because it is bogged down in the finite. In such cases, the man is not a romantic, but rather a philistine or a petty bourgeois. Actually, alienation appears the moment negativity disappears from consciousness. Be it a romanticist's or a philistine's, in both cases consciousness is alienated from its own nature, for it lacks the harmonious interplay between the finite and the infinite which negativity sets off. This interplay loses force and may even stop as soon as one is positively attached either to the infinite or to the finite. Thus there are these two ways in which consciousness is alienated from its own nature, and Kierkegaard describes them at length in *The Sickness unto Death*. In part, it is the dispersion of man in the infinite, in abstract possibles:

> Possibility then appears to the self ever greater and greater, more and more things become possible, because nothing becomes actual. At last it is as if everything were possible—but this is precisely when the abyss has swallowed up the self. Every little possibility even would require some time to become actuality. But finally the time which should be available for actuality becomes shorter and shorter, everything becomes more and more instantaneous. Possibility becomes more and more intense—but only in the sense of possibility, not in the sense of actuality; for in the sense of actuality the meaning of intensity is that at least something of that which is possible becomes actual. At the instant something appears possible, and then a new possibility makes its appearance, at last this phantasmagoria moves so rapidly that it is as if everything were possible—and this is precisely the last moment, when the individual becomes for himself a mirage.[2]

Nothing becomes "actual" in the immanence of the esthet-

85

icist. Consciousness has no objects. Generally, the "actual" is a synthesis, formed when the possible, i.e., the phenomenon, upon its emergence, finds in consciousness a continuity or frame of reference that gives it meaning. But this does not happen by itself. Man must be an agent and must cause that synthesis. In other words, man must be attentive to it. We have already seen that this is true of the ethicist whose reflective and articulated capacities constitute a meaningful world and person for him. It is this continuity which is lacking in the esthetic immanence, and that is why no "actuality" forms in it. Neither world nor person flow forth. To the estheticist, everything seems possible, fortuitous, and senseless, and he wonders: "Where am I? What does the world mean?" and so on. Ordinary phenomena are arrayed around him, and he cannot decipher them. As a matter of fact, he does not even want to do so, for he is either dreaming, or diverted, or sunk in some mood or other. His consciousness has no roots and no objects.

The philistine's consciousness, like the estheticist's, is also alienated. However, it loses itself in the succession of things rather than in an abstraction from them. The philistine is bogged down and dulled in finiteness, and his spiritual life lacks the horizon of infinity:

> Despairing narrowness consists in the lack of primitiveness, or of the fact one has deprived oneself of one's primitiveness; it consists in having emasculated oneself, in a spiritual sense. . . . While one sort of despair plunges wildly into the infinite and loses itself, a second sort permits itself as it were to be defrauded by "the others." By seeing the multitude of men about it, by getting engaged in all sorts of worldly affairs, by becoming wise about how things go in this world, such a man forgets himself,

forgets what his name is (in the divine understanding of it), does not dare to believe in himself, finds it too venturesome a thing to be himself, far easier and safer to be like the others, to become an imitation, a number, a cipher in the crowd.[3]

Both the estheticist and the philistine take their own ideational construct to be actual reality, never feeling the tug of a "beyond" or of transcendence. The contents of their lives appear positive and real to them, and they are satisfied with the deceptive certainty, or at least the temporary relief, offered by the worldly life. They have no bifurcation, no split, no "is" and "ought," dividing their energies and energizing their laggard ways.

Kierkegaard deals with alienation also in an essay originally published as a review, entitled in English *The Present Age*. Speaking of his own time, Kierkegaard describes the general tendency of his contemporaries to lose themselves in abstractions and become petrified in sterile and never ending calculations. In an unspontaneous and passionless age, even a person contemplating suicide cannot bring himself to decide on it. He considers the matter, subjects it to endless deliberations, and even if he finally dies, it would not be said that he really committed suicide, but rather that the deliberation took his life away from him.[4] Instead of becoming involved in the possibles offered by thought (and involvement here means choosing, while at the same time overcoming, one possibility, and thus putting oneself into a never-ending process and movement of becoming), the alienated man gives up on himself and identifies himself haphazardly with each emerging occasion, to the point where the happenings strangle him and turn him into a nonentity. In this unspontaneous attitude of the age, Kierke-

gaard says, the individual has almost disappeared. Instead of speaking of the individual, one speaks of "the public." The individual can no longer be himself, and he submits to what the public believes or says. But the public is only a conceptual abstraction, a "phantom," a "monstrous nothing" that levels the individual to a nothing. The public is happy to make fun of individuals and submit them to this leveling process, and it is aided in this by the press. Kierkegaard likens the press to a dog that the public lets loose against the individual.[5] And the individual, too weak to resist, allows himself to be conquered and loses himself within the anonymous public. He gives up everything that is "primitive" (i.e., original) in himself, and thus becomes a "man," to use a Heideggerian term, but not a true individual.

In this connection, let us consider a case of alienation that Kierkegaard describes in *Postscript*:

> I shall here permit myself to tell a story, which without any sort of adaptation on my part comes direct from an asylum. A patient in such an institution seeks to escape, and actually succeeds in effecting his purpose by leaping out of a window, and prepares to start on the road to freedom, when the thought strikes him (shall I say sanely enough or madly enough?): "When you come to town you will be recognized, and you will at once be brought back here again; hence you need to prepare yourself fully to convince everyone by the objective truth of what you say, that all is in order as far as your sanity is concerned." As he walks along and thinks about this, he sees a ball lying on the ground, picks it up, and puts in into the tail pocket of his coat. Every step he takes the ball strikes him, politely speaking, on his hinder parts, and every time it thus strikes him he says: "Bang, the earth is round." He

comes to the city, and at once calls on one of his friends; he wants to convince him that he is not crazy, and therefore walks back and forth, saying continually: "Bang, the earth is round!"[6]

Who could dispute the fact that the earth is round? Nonetheless, we have an alienated man before us. The sentence "the earth is round" is a conceptual characterization, the value of which is determined in a well-defined frame of reference. If the earth were this frame, the characterization would have some sense. But the madman has changed the frame of reference, or, what amounts to the same thing, he has chosen a characterization which does not do what he wants it to do. Instead of proving his mental health, the "objective truth"—that the world is round—actually demonstrates his insanity. It does not take the doctor very long to see this, says Kierkegaard, adding: "But all men are not physicians. . . ." Man has a tendency to disguise his insanity with "objective truths" of all sorts, and he often does this so cleverly that nobody has any suspicions. The truth is that the story of the madman told by Kierkegaard applies to all of us. For as soon as we are born, our environment, in a thousand conscious and unconscious ways, inculcates in us a complex system of reference consisting of value and motivational judgments. We adopt norms that we consider "objective" and even unshakable, and we conform to a multitude of rules of conduct that we pretend are absolute. In fact there is nothing absolute about these norms, and they often serve as a surrogate, concealing man's lack of inwardness.

The alienated man adapts himself to norms, either social or religious, not because he realizes their values, but merely through habit. In his works Kierkegaard incessantly criti-

cizes habit as the sort of mental paralysis that turns man into a machine. And he lashes out especially against Christians who are Christian by habit. *The Instant*, a number of pamphlets he published in 1855, abounds in descriptions of these; and, as a matter of fact, the "pseudobeliever" is a subject Kierkegaard deals with constantly. Here is an example from *The Concept of Dread*:

> A partisan of the most rigid orthodoxy may be demoniacal. He knows it all, he bows before the holy, truth is for him an ensemble of ceremonies, he talks about presenting himself before the throne of God, of how many times one must bow, he knows everything the same way as does the pupil who is able to demonstrate a mathematical proposition with the letters ABC, but not when they are changed to DEF. He is therefore in dread whenever he hears something not arranged in the same order. And yet how closely he resembles a modern speculative philosopher who found out a new proof for the immortality of the soul, then came into mortal danger and could not produce his proof because he had not his notebooks with him.[7]

The alienated man loses more and more of his vitality and finally becomes an object that can be manipulated mechanically. This mechanical aspect is clearly shown in the description of the madman we have quoted. Note the repetitive way that the ball strikes the madman's posterior. Note also the tiresome repetition of "the earth is round" and the movement of the madman from one end of the room to the other, quite like the movement of a pendulum. In *The Present Age*, already mentioned, Kierkegaard compares his own generation to a clock that no longer works very well. Instead of chiming twelve times at noon and once at one

o'clock, this clock always chimes only once at fixed intervals throughout the day.[8] The alienated man is an object, not a living synthesis.

But it seems as though the alienated man likes his state of alienation. Modeling himself on the norms that the public has set for him, he finds a reassuring atmosphere of social habits which absolve him of all personal responsibility. The mechanical way of life seems stable and long lived to him. He is then afraid of losing the security provided by the beaten path; even if it leads to a dead end, even if he suspects something uncertain about it, he wants to convince himself at all cost that everything is all right. The alienated man *insists* on remaining in his alienation. In *Judge for Yourselves!*, Kierkegaard writes:

For the true situation is this. We men are all of us more or less drunken. But with us it is as with a man who is full, but not entirely full, so that he has not lost consciousness, no, he has just the consciousness that he is slightly full, and just for this reason he is careful to hide this from others, if possible from himself. What does he do then? He seeks something to hold on to, thus he walks close to the houses, and so walks straight without turning dizzy— a sober man. But across an open square he will not venture to walk, for thus it would be revealed, what he himself knows, that he is full. So it is, spiritually understood, with us men. We have a suspicion of ourselves, we know fairly well within ourselves that we are not thoroughly sober. But then shrewdness and common sense and discretion come to our aid, so that by this help we can get something to hold on to—the finite. And then we walk straight and with confidence, without turning dizzy—we are entirely sober. But in case the absolute were absolute-

ly to cast a glance at us (yet from this glance we with-draw, it is for this reason we hide among finite things, as Adam hid among the trees), or in case we were to cast a glance infinitely at the infinite (yet we keep ourselves from doing this, it is for this reason we busily employ our eyes upon errands in the service of finitude)—in case the absolute were to cast a glance at us or we at it, then it would be revealed that we are drunk. Such is the true sit-uation. But in our thieves' [cant] (Tyvesprog) we men express it differently, we maintain that we are shrewd, sensible, and discreet persons, that we are sober, and that it is precisely the absolute which would intoxicate us. This is as if that drunken man were to say, "I am sober; but if I were to walk across a large square, that large square would make me drunk."[9]

It is with the help of captious reasoning that the alien-ated man seeks to affirm himself at all cost, and he finds enough ambiguities in the use of language to make this pos-sible. Note that Kierkegaard considers our daily patois to be "thieves' cant," and this is an important point in his re-flection. In *The Present Age*, he sees chitchat as an essential trait of his contemporaries,[10] and in *The Concept of Dread* he gives us a revealing description of this:

> In fact, spirit-lessness can utter the same words the rich-est spirit has uttered, only it does not utter them by virtue of spirit. Man when he is characterized as spirit-less has become a talking-machine, and there is nothing to pre-vent him from learning a philosophical rigmarole just as easily as a confession of faith and a political recitative repeated by rote.[11]

Kierkegaard views chitchat as "doing away with the vital

distinction between talking and keeping silent," and also as "doing away with the distinction between private affairs and public ones." Chitchat results from the fact that the alienated man lends himself to trivialities, to conceptual ambiguities in which the qualitative distinctions that differentiate the individual from the public disappear. Kierkegaard points out the fact that the reflections of his contemporaries tend to abolish the law of contradiction, upon which all qualitative distinctions are based. And it is our language, our thieves' cant, which lends support to chitchat and thus constitutes a social factor in securing the alienation of consciousness from the truly human ends.

It will be easy to see the reason for this if we return to the structure of human consciousness. Consciousness celebrates the tension between the particular and the general. Even when one sees a black dot on a white surface, for example, dialectical tension between the dot and the background upon which it appears is made possible by the complexities of consciousness. Now the term "dot" is not expressive of this tension, but it alone gives us a perverted and false picture of conscious activity. While in consciousness the positive is balanced by the negative, in our language, linguistic terms seem all positive—they are what they are. Enumerating only what transpires immediately, language lends the false impression that there are only "positive givens." It cannot express the "either/or," i.e., the dialectical tension constantly developing in consciousness. Language is, by itself, thus a thief robbing us of the real character of the activities of our consciousness. As dialectical tension subsides in the alienated immanence, as the distinction between the particular and the general is blurred in it, becoming preoccupied with language only accelerates the process of alienation, since it makes man forget the "either/or," the

tension, of his active conscious life. It is in language that the alienated man finds abstract ambiguities, and he makes use of chitchat to disguise his alienation. In the *Journals*, Kierkegaard writes:

> . . . Whoever is clever at listening to people talk also discovers the deceit which exists because the words are not connected to definite thoughts. This is not demonstrated when one hears a single word, but as soon as one hears it with other words. The most naive man can say: God exists, a child also pronounces the name of God. Nevertheless, it would be a fair judgement to say that connecting a definite thought to a word is a task which demands the most extreme efforts on the part of the thinker. I could write pages and pages if I wanted to show through examples that people speak in such a way that their own words prove that they are not thinking of anything.[12]

The form of linguistic expression does not correspond to the conscious activity. That is why conscious experience, demonstrating the dialectical relation between the general and the particular, cannot be exhaustively expressed in language. This applies to the esthetic stage of life as well, insofar as that stage also includes dialectical experiences. The esthete Don Juan, in which, as we have seen, this dialectical relation operates, can find expression only in music.[13] Nor can ethical life be represented only by words, even poetic words.[14] Conscious life has no surrogates—it must be lived. The inward life of the ethicist, Kierkegaard tells us, is expressed in terms of life and not in terms of language. The same thing is true of the religious life. Abraham kept silent during his journey to Mount Moriah, and like him, every believer is silent during his inward dialogue with God. No words can substitute for a Christian's love. In *Works of Love*, Kierkegaard writes:

There is no word in human language, not a single one, not the most sacred word, of which we could say: when a man uses this word, it is unconditionally proved thereby that there is love in him. Rather, it is true that a word from one person can convince us that there is love in him and the opposite word from another can convince that there is love in him also. It is true that one and the same word can convince us that love dwells in the person who uttered it and not in another who nevertheless uttered the same word.[15]

The deeper the inwardness, the more man loves silence. And, conversely, the more a man speaks and talks, the more he lacks inwardness.*

Having noted the limit of language and the nature of chitchat, we shall now consider the demoniacal, which is still another example of alienation. We have already seen that the demoniacal man is characterized by inward closure which Kierkegaard also calls "shut-upness" or hardening of oneself. Enclosed in his own self, the demoniacal man avoids all sorts of communication. He does not speak. Despite the fact that language relative to consciousness is an abstraction that cannot adequately render its content, language is nevertheless a means of liberation, for it provides one's consciousness with some sort of articulation, however imperfect:

The shut-up is precisely the mute; the spoken word is precisely the saving thing, that which delivers from the mute abstraction of the shut-up.[16]

The demoniacal man does not wish to speak, not because he possesses a deep inwardness which does not lend itself to the articulations of language, but because he is bogged

* Author's note: This is of course not true of indirect communication which will be dealt with in the following chapter.

95

down and does not want to open up. The immanence of the demoniacal man expresses itself rather in mechanical, sudden, and brusque movements. Kierkegaard writes:

> Hence the aptness of the demoniacal for the mimic art, not in the sense of the beautiful but of the sudden, the abrupt, something which life often gives us opportunity to observe.[17]

Other characteristics of the demoniacal man are, according to Kierkegaard, exaggerated sensibility, exaggerated irritability, nervous affections, hysteria, and hypochondria.[18] But the demoniacal is above all "unfreedom which would shut itself off"[19] and also a deep "dread of the good." We have already seen that freedom is actually that good which operates in the opening up of man, in his coming-out-of-himself. But the demoniacal man is attached to whatever he already is, and does not want to be free. Note that what we have here is *dread* of the good, and according to Kierkegaard, dread is a dialectical category. It, too, is describable by concepts. In *The Concept of Dread*, Kierkegaard deals with dread by relating it to the state of innocence in which Adam lived before eating the fruit of the tree of knowledge. The innocence of Adam, says Kierkegaard, was not entirely a state of calm and relaxation. He writes:

> In this state there is peace and repose; but at the same time there is something different, which is not dissension and strife, for there is nothing to strive with. What is it then? Nothing. But what effect does nothing produce? It begets dread. This is the profound secret of innocence, that at the same time it is dread.[20]

Kierkegaard explains: In innocence, he says, man is not yet determined as spirit; his soul is in immediate unity with

his natural being.[21] He does not make himself his own object; he does not think about himself. He is not conscious in any specific sense. In the state of innocence the potential for spirituality exists only in an immediate fashion. In other words, in the state of innocence we do not yet have a clear articulation differentiating the three components of consciousness from each other. Nonetheless, the spirit exists in it, though somnolent. It is dreaming, says Kierkegaard, and he adds:

> When awake, the difference between myself and my other is posited; sleeping, it is suspended; dreaming, it is a nothing vaguely hinted at. The reality of the spirit constantly shows itself in a form which entices its possibility, but it is away as soon as one grasps after it, and it is a nothing which is able only to alarm.[22]

It is the possibility of awakening the spirit which produces dread. This possibility continually haunts Adam's state of innocence, because he is aware of the prohibition which forbids him the fruit of the tree of knowledge. This prohibition, says Kierkegaard, disturbs Adam because it hints at the possibility of freedom which would bring the stirring of the spirit in its wake. Naturally, in the state of innocence, Adam does not yet understand the meaning of this prohibition. But the prohibition sets the possibility of "being able" in motion in him. He knows that he can act, that he can accept or reject something and thus exercise his freedom. Now, dread is precisely this freedom as possibility. "There is only the possibility of being able, as a higher form of ignorance, as a heightened expression of dread, because this in a more profound sense is and is not, because in a more profound sense he [Adam] loves it and flees from it."[23] Adam is alarmed by the possibility of being able, he is

97

afraid of it at the same time that he loves it. The freedom which he experiences is still a trammeled one, and the spirit in him is still only a nothing, though real enough to tempt him. The dread produced by the possibility of being able is therefore dialectical; it is a fear with an indefinite object, as well as an agreeable temptation, a titillation. Kierkegaard considers dread to be both sympathetic antipathy and antipathetic sympathy.[24]

Kierkegaard's observations on dread bring us back to the demoniacal which Kierkegaard considers to entail the dread of the good. The demoniacal man is in an opposing relationship with the good or with the state of opening. He has prohibited himself from opening up, but at the same time he knows that he is capable of coming out of himself. Here we have what Kierkegaard calls the dialectical character of the demoniacal dread of the good. The demoniacal man is not free, for he is shut off from the liberty which constantly impinges upon him. By a sort of spite or rejection, the demoniacal man renounces the freedom which impinges upon him and shuts himself off. Somehow, he feels the opening up—freedom—but he fears it at the same time. Torn by dread, he preys upon his own heart by absorbing himself in abstract and infinite reflections. The diary called "Guilty/Not Guilty," which is part of *Stages on Life's Way*, presents the lifeless calculations and thoughts of a person who thinks and dreams of his beloved without having any real contact with her. Kierkegaard considers him a demoniacal man.[25]

Any positive attachment to the immediate and given way of the world is an instance of man's alienation, and in this state of alienation, he becomes only an object, or a body. The body is the fall of man, for originally man was not a body but a spirit:

. . . the body is an organ of the soul, and thus in turn of the spirit. So soon as the subordinate relationship comes to an end, so soon as the body revolts, so soon as freedom enters into a conspiracy with it against itself, there unfreedom is present as the demoniacal.[26]

As soon as a man attaches himself to what already is, that appears to him to be the reality and a positive object. In this way man himself becomes a body, or another object, reducing himself to whatever he already is. He loses the teleological thrust that an obligation or duty, a divine uneasiness, would produce. This state is precisely the fall of man:

> The idea of Christianity is that man is a fallen spirit; and just as in Russia, for example, when an aristocrat has done wrong, he is punished by being thrust into the army as an ordinary soldier, in the same way, a fallen spirit is punished by being thrust into that slave set-up which is the body, he is sent into the penitentiary which is the world because of his sins. . . .[27]

We shall see in the ninth chapter of this work that Christianity actually aims at *dematerializing* the everyday world by transforming man into spirit. So powerful is the human consciousness that in the nonalienated consciousness, emerging phenomena are never simply treated as material things. For the Christian, the phenomena are only "signs," in which the soul discovers meaning. Man as spirit never allows the phenomenal world to become fixed or transformed into a skein of objects. Because he keeps his distance in virtue of a new consciousness, he is always receptive to the novelties, and he is thus open, too, to the manifestations of God. But the alienated man sticks to the immediate, which becomes the positive thing, and it acts as an opaque veil

which hides transcendence and thus traps him into sinfulness. Each emerging phenomenon is proof of the fall of man, and it is up to every man to struggle constantly against the immediate so that he may attain a transcendent existence through faith and thus be transformed into a spirit. But if man insists on remaining in the immediate, if he encloses himself in the environment, he thereby becomes an object. We have already noted this mechanical aspect of the alienated man's behavior.

These remarks on alienation have shown us to what degree man is averse to resignation. Through acquired habit or through spite, man remains closed in upon himself. Kierkegaard is well aware of the temptations which attract man to a state of alienation, if only because of the anonymity that this state offers, and which man seeks in order to forget himself. The fact is that nobody ever escapes these temptations entirely, and there is always a lurking corner that attracts man and enjoins him to stay there. For example, the humorist, though he does not attach himself to any one immediately given thing, nevertheless withdraws by exercising his power of conceiving everything as affording a joke. He takes his pleasure where he can find it and also circumscribes the development of his consciousness, even with his talent for humor. Therefore, one has only to laugh in this manner in order to stop being a believer. The fact that one speaks in trivialities may also be an obstacle in the path that leads to faith. One can escape alienation only in Christianity, for Christianity demands a total self-renunciation that abolishes any residual reliance upon one's immanental capacities. To be sure, considering the obstacles and temptations, it is not easy to become a Christian. But what one can do is struggle against oneself, against one's own alienation, in order to become one. And this is a perpetual struggle, an

effort that is more and more prolonged, for one is never completely Christian.

Let us stress that the Christianity described by Kierkegaard is far from being a prescription requiring man to live in isolation from the everyday world. Renouncing the immediate does not mean choosing the monastic life, and Kierkegaard comes out categorically against a life of that kind. Accordingly, Christianity calls on man to live in the immediate while simultaneously giving it up. We have already seen that Christianity supposes self-love; however, it affirms this while demanding the extension of equal love to others. Christianity only seeks to reestablish the true nature, or rather the proper functioning, of consciousness, since in a healthy consciousness, the finite person affirms himself while negating himself. One must continue living in the world while keeping one's distance from it, and thus one is free to receive what God is constantly revealing.

To conclude this discussion, we shall briefly note the Genesis story of Lot and the cities of Sodom and Gomorrah. As Kierkegaard likes to utilize Biblical stories to express his ideas, we have chosen the Sodom and Gomorrah story in order to illustrate, by means of a parable, Kierkegaard's observations on alienation.

The Bible tale relates that God rained fire and sulphur on the two cities in order to destroy them. Lot, who was a just and God-fearing man, was saved; the angels sent him away from Sodom before they destroyed it. As they were leaving the town, Lot's wife looked back, and became a pillar of salt.

It should be noted that Lot hesitated to leave the town, although he knew God's decision and despite the angels' promise to save him. The story says that the angels made Lot leave, by leading him by the hand. One should not be

astonished at Lot's hesitation, which is after all a very natural response. Nothing in the story leads us to believe that Lot hated his fellow citizens. As a believer, he doubtless had compassion for the sinners around him, especially when he knew God's decision. Besides, Lot loved the region where he lived and where he had spent a considerable part of his life. Suddenly he was forced to renounce that part of his life and leave behind everything he had built. Lot hesitated, and doubtless said to himself: "It's better to die." Fortunately, there were angels to force him to leave the city. At the moment of departure, Lot was ready to accept any future and begin his life anew, but his wife looked back and turned into a pillar of salt.

Here we have the image that can exemplify the alienation of man. As soon as one refuses to reject the immediate and live towards the unknown, one is fixed and becomes one more thing—a pillar of salt. If man *insists* on remaining in what already is, he cannot *exist* as a person. Transcendence, as well as the other depth factors, stays hidden from him as a result of the fact that he does not exercise the richness of consciousness, that he is an object or a body and not a spirit. One begins to become spirit when one comes out of oneself and realizes a potential. Just as Lot awaited another future outside of Sodom, man must strive to be something that he is not at the moment. He must await the emergence of new phenomena, a new self, as well as the grace that will reveal transcendent existence to him. Since, however, this leave-taking, this resignation, often demands enormous efforts—and the hesitations of Lot are a token of them—man has need of some outside help in order to operate. He cannot count on the angels to help; he now has only one recourse: communication with others. This can help man renounce the immediate and thus save him from self-aliena-

tion. And, therefore, we must turn to Kierkegaard's reflections about how men do in fact stand in communal relations
one with another. That these relations help a man to full
consciousness and full selfhood will be the burden of our
discussion of the limits and possibilities of communication
to which we now turn.

7.

Consciousness and the Uses of Irony and Humor

To CLARIFY Kierkegaard's theory of communication, we should like to address two questions. At first glance, these questions might cast doubt on Kierkegaard's philosophical ideas, and consequently, also on our thesis. After dealing with them, however, we shall see that Kierkegaard is well aware of the problems that these questions raise, and that his philosophy provides a solution to them.

The first question is the following: how can one speak of a particular and transcendent being if one knows only the perceived phenomena which hide it? How can one state that such a being exists? It is clear that a direct statement has no philosophical and cognitive value. Does Kierkegaard's philosophy conform to the fundamental rule of all philosophical reasoning—that it shall be consistent in the exposition of its ideas? Kierkegaard emphasizes countless times that "existence" is not a concept, that it does not become a concept, and that it cannot be thought. Nonetheless, Kierkegaard thinks about it, speaks of it, and acknowledges its real existence. Is this not contradictory? How can one state the existence of some unknown thing that is neither a phenomenon nor a concept?

It will be said that Kierkegaard does not mean to demonstrate philosophically "the existence" of existence, for that

104

would be contradictory; on the contrary, he wants to say that the acknowledgement of existence is attained in faith and not through any kind of philosophical reasoning. It is true that according to Kierkegaard one "believes" in existence and attains it by means of the religious leap. But the philosophy of Kierkegaard would have little value if its only aim was to tell us that transcendent existence is the object of faith, and that one cannot "know" God, but only believe in Him. Kierkegaard's works would still have a very considerable literary value, for his genius in this respect is undeniable. But if we adhere to rigid intellectual criteria in examining Kierkegaard's ideas, we cannot refrain from challenging his findings in regard to transcendent existence. A consistent philosopher would not even have stated that existence is something encompassed noncognitively through faith, for this direct statement concerning existence establishes, though negatively, that existence is thus grasped. Such a philosopher would have preferred silence, thereby preserving philosophical consistency. But Kierkegaard does not keep silent; he speaks constantly through his works. Nonetheless, Kierkegaard is far from being inconsistent. We shall see that he actually does maintain a kind of silence in regard to existence. For transcendent existence is ineffable.

The second question that we should like to pose is the following: Is the philosophy of Kierkegaard solipsistic? At first glance, everything gives this impression. The other, as we have seen, only is an internal determinant of man's very consciousness when it is taken up by that consciousness. Now if I thus carry within myself the other, as well as the other phenomena of which I am aware, does an "outside" exist for me? It is true that the "outside" exists, and that, as Kierkegaard says, it is aggrandized through faith. But it is equally true that so long as man is not a believer, he does

not know this outside. He does not even know whether God exists or whether his own immanence was created by a factor that exists outside himself. In the *Journals*, Kierkegaard writes:

> Consciousness presupposes itself, and to wonder at its origin is an idle question, as captious as that of the Ancients: which came first, the tree or the acorn? Without an acorn, where would the first tree have come from? And without a tree, whence then the first acorn?[1]

This actually brings us back to our first question, and it is clear that man, as a conscious being, does not know, directly, anything outside of himself. This raises another question in regard to "the other," the things outside of himself. At the end of the last chapter, we said that the other can save man from alienation, and this seems to presuppose that the other exists outside of man. But if man does not know directly these things, and the other is merely an internal determinant of personal consciousness, then how can the other save man from alienation? Perhaps, of course, the world is known indirectly, via consciousness and its components, but is not, therefore, only itself within consciousness. These are the issues we shall examine in Kierkegaard's theory of communication.

The philosophy of Kierkegaard concerns itself with two orders of external things. On the one hand there is that which we shall call "the historical other," and on the other hand that which we shall describe as "the transhistorical other." The first when it exists in personal consciousness is no more than a "possible," which, as a possible, is learned through direct communication. The transhistorical other, however, requires indirect communication, which constitutes a thrust backward experienced by personal conscious-

ness. There is an actual presence that produces the thrust backwards, and for this reason it is transhistorical.

By "direct communication," Kierkegaard means any conveyance of positive facts. Such a communication always is about something, some "object"; it is a piece of information.[2] The mathematical sciences, for example, are communication of this sort, as are logic and history. In every case we are purveying also information, and it should be stressed that the facts communicated by the information are always abstract. Direct communication is completely indifferent to the immanent reality of man and incapable of rendering it adequately. Logic is no more than relationships between abstract concepts; it is a closed system which, Kierkegaard stresses, cannot encompass or express the temporal movement of reality. On the other hand, objective history never rises above the level of the possible. Napoleon is no more than a configuration of possibles, an object that changes constantly with the addition of each new historical detail. No direct communication or account can represent the living presence of a man, whether of Napoleon, or even of a man still alive. Furthermore, we have seen that language cannot adequately express immanence. Historical science is, then, a quantitative approximation that collects all possible historical details in order to come close to reality.[3] But it never attains this reality, and for us Napoleon will always remain a more or less abstract historical fact—a possible.

In *Postscript*, Kierkegaard says that direct communication, in matters of morals and religion, is not communication at all,[4] and it is very important to note this point. Direct communication, says Kierkegaard, supposes an awareness only of its content. It is an objective thought which is interested in positive facts, without acknowledging the subjec-

tive inwardness and the dialectical tension of this inwardness in which the positive is expressed by the negative. This brings us back to the subject of solipsism. Real communication presupposes, even as indicated by the etymological sense of the term, a relationship between at least two persons. Now one always learns positive facts through the senses, and these senses, of themselves, do not reveal any presence existing outside of oneself. It therefore makes very little difference whether I learn facts by reading a book, or by listening to someone who is speaking to me directly, or even by witnessing the occurrence of events myself. The "fact" is what I learn. It is always within myself that I bear the facts. To construe that fact as a revelation of the world and others is another act of the subject, another feat of consciousness. It is thus clear that in direct communication there is no question of an actual relationship between two or among several persons. There is only a single person—myself. I must make of it what I can.

But direct communication does not require even the existence of a single person. It is basically completely impersonal, for the very reason that it communicates objective givens. Objectivity is anonymous. It is an arbitrary fixation of phenomena that sums up the phenomenal world in concepts. One says, for instance: there is a tree. A complex of data or rather a variety of phenomena are congealed in the single term "tree." This term, which makes a direct communication, does not express anything particular, or anything characteristic. Any objective fact is merely obscure opaqueness, or abstraction without articulation. Direct communication "fills" my immanental capacities with objective facts, and it does so by giving the erroneous impression that these facts are reality itself. In this way personal consciousness itself becomes more and more objective, to the

point where it disappears in an objective opaqueness. Man is then turned into a robot operated by acquired habits and concepts which disregard the person and his inwardness. Kierkegaard's observations on alienation have given us examples of this. In direct communication we do not have a person who communicates, nor necessarily a person who receives the communication. It only requires a voice who says things. That is why this type of communication is not really communication. It is simply the actual emergence of new phenomena, which are impersonal, since they are only themselves, and which consequently suppose no subjectivity. They are otherwise unrelated. According to the philosophy of Kierkegaard, direct communication evinces not only solipsism, but also, if one can express it thus, impersonal solipsism.

In the light of these observations, a question arises. Assuming that man tends to identify himself positively with the immediate, what then creates in him this negative articulation which dissipates objective opaqueness? What brings about a change? When and how will he attain the reflective stage in which the immediate is vanquished in order to foster that consciousness which will let the historical other be found? We have seen that reflection develops in the ethical stage of life in which a conscious relationship between man and the historical other is established. But one is not born a reflective man, and we have already seen the cases where esthetic consciousness has no objects, where it only floats, since it is a mood, or a dream, or a fanciful thought. For the newborn as well, the world is but a single piece and color. What is it then that introduces qualitative articulation into personal consciousness? Is it the world itself? Kierkegaard wants his reader to understand both that the change in consciousness is required in order to have the qualitative dif-

ferences noted, but that this does not mean that the changes are only in the subject, not in the objective world. We shall see that the articulation of consciousness comes about also because of the action of the transhistorical other. This exists outside personal consciousness, and it provokes a shock in consciousness that gives birth to reflection. Thus men do experience the existence of external things, and one is not confined to a solipsism. The transhistorical other always requires indirect communication, and according to Kierkegaard such communications are via irony, humor, art, and even Christianity.

In *Training in Christianity*, Kierkegaard considers indirect communication under a "sign of contradiction." Jesus is such a sign (Luke 2:34). A communication where joking and seriousness are combined is, while apparently contradictory, also a deep and indirect kind of communication.[5] Before considering, in the following chapter, Kierkegaard's observations on Jesus as a sign of contradiction, we shall here consider types of indirect communication in which the amusing and the serious are combined, namely irony and humor.

At the outset, Kierkegaard explains the meaning of the term "sign" in order to make clear what he means by the term "a sign of contradiction," which he uses later. He says that a sign is a negation of immediacy, or "a second state of being, differing from the first."[6] A nautical signal is, for instance, a sign. It has to be interpreted. From the immediate point of view it is certainly something—a post, a light, etc.—but not a sign, for as a sign it is something other than what it immediately appears to be. A sign, then, is an object which mediates something.

Kierkegaard also explains what he means by "a sign of contradiction":

A "sign of contradiction" is a sign which contains in itself a contradiction. There is no contradiction in the fact that a thing is immediately this or that and at the same time a sign; for something there must be immediately existing to serve as a sign; where there is literally nothing there is no sign. On the other hand, a sign of contradiction is a sign which contains in its very constitution a contradiction. To justify the name of "sign" there must be something whereby it draws attention to itself or to the contradiction. But the contradictions contained in it must not be such as to cancel the two terms and bring the sign to naught, nor must it be such that the sign becomes the opposite of a sign, an absolute secret.—A communication which is the unity of jest and earnest is such a sign of contradiction.[7]

We now understand one thing: an indirect communication does not convey a simple fact to us. It elicits from us, on the contrary, something else than what it plainly says by producing a feeling of contradiction in us. Since it is a sign of contradiction, this thing cannot be an "object" or a definite fact. However, it is not a nothing either. Kierkegaard adds:

Indirect communication can be produced by the art of reduplicating the communication. This art consists in reducing oneself, the communicator, to nobody, something purely objective, and then incessantly composing qualitative opposites into unity. This is what some of the pseudonyms [behind which Kierkegaard himself hid] are accustomed to call "double reflection." An example of such indirect communication is, so to compose jest and earnest that the composition is a dialectical knot—and with this

111

to be nobody. If anyone is to profit by this sort of communication, he must himself undo the knot for himself.[8]

We have just learned that indirect communication establishes a union of qualitative opposites, a sign of contradiction, and that the communicator reduces himself to nobody, i.e., while he is communicating he disappears completely. Someone says a contradictory thing and disappears at the same time. Kierkegaard says that this constitutes a double reflection, and he explains in *Postscript*:

> The form of a communication must be distinguished from its expression. When the thought has found its suitable expression in the word, which is realized by means of a first reflection, there follows a second reflection, concerned with the relation between the communication and the author of it, and reflecting the author's own existential relationship to the Idea.[9]

The medium of communication must be distinguished from its form. In this case the medium is ordinary words and sentences. The first reflection consists of choosing the words and saying something with them. The second reflection is to assure the relationship between the statement and the one who makes it. For the statement is an indirect communication and supposes both the statement and something else. It requires another kind of activity of the reader or hearer than simply believing the statement. And to get this requirement it must be done indirectly. The relationship between the statement and its maker is highly dialectical. The communicator withdraws and hides behind his statement, unwilling to identify himself with it. On the other hand, the statement itself is a union of several qualitative opposites—it may even be a sign of contradiction. We are

not dealing here with a purely logical contradiction that is reduced to nothing, but rather with something more like a combination of contraries. In indirect communication, three things happen at the same time: one affirms something, one suggests something different, even contrary, and in doing so, one disappears himself leaving the issues to the hearer.

According to Kierkegaard, irony is an example of indirect communication in which jest and earnest are combined. To say something ironically is to introduce another factor by one's manner. Let us analyze an ironic reply that Kierkegaard reports in *Postscript* and that will permit us to penetrate Kierkegaard's observation on irony: Someone has approached an ironist in order to confide a secret to him. The ironist replies that he can be relied upon completely to keep a secret because he will "forget it as quickly as it is uttered."[10]

The ironist is asked to keep a secret, and he promises to forget it. Let us note, however, that the verb "forget" in this case does something very odd with the meaning of the verb "keep." But it does so in denying it. When one forgets a secret, one keeps it well; however, one does not keep it if one forgets it. The ironic reply is thus oddly a contradictory sign and it produces an uncertainty in the hearer. In *The Concept of Irony*, Kierkegaard writes:

> In oratorical discourse there frequently occurs a figure of speech which bears the name of irony and whose characteristic is this: to say the opposite of what is meant. With this we already have a determination present in all forms of irony, namely, the phenomenon is not the essence but the opposite of the essence. When I speak the thought or meaning is the essence, the word the phenomenon. These two moments are absolutely necessary, and

113

it is in this sense that Plato has remarked that all thinking is dialogue. Now truth demands identity, for if I have the thought without the word, I do not have the thought; and if I have the word without the thought, I do not have the word, since it may not be said that infants and the demented speak. When next I consider the speaking subject, I again have a determination present in all forms of irony, namely, the subject is negatively free.[11]

Irony exploits the incommensurability of the essence of certain kinds of thoughts in relation to whatever they are about. The ironic reply which we have analyzed above accentuates simultaneously both the difference and the resemblance between the two verbs, "keep" and "forget." Before understanding this reply, one has believed that "forget" expresses a certain conscious activity which is incompatible with the meaning ordinarily imparted to the verb "keep." The ironic reply in question reveals the insufficiency of language as a means of expression and thus makes the hearer mistrustful of the ordinary meaning of an asseveration. One really wants trust and confidence and honesty. Any word will be different from that. The hearer now knows that "keep" does not entirely express the dialectical significance of the activities involved in being trustful and that it is incapable of doing so. It is therefore necessary, he tells himself, to find another verb or to create another expression to render this dialectical activity. And the same thing is true in regard to the term "confide." Because of the ironic reply, the hearer wonders whether his ironic friend's behavior justifies confiding in him. Is this friend a confidant or not? Perhaps one must redefine what one ordinarily means by "confidant?" In any case, the ironic reply forces the hearer to detach himself from the ordinary meaning of words and

human relations, although it does not substitute anything new for the ordinary meaning. Indirect communication begins, says Kierkegaard, with a recoil; it is a thrust backward (Tilbagestød) which pushes the hearer into deeper self-reflection.[12] The ironist frees himself from the scene and his hearer, too, not only by what he says, but mostly by how he says it. His communication is guarded by a manner that puts it into another light.

In *The Concept of Irony*, Kierkegaard describes at length the ways in which the ironist denies while apparently agreeing. One of these is by exaggeration. For instance, in the face of stupid and insipid enthusiasm, Kierkegaard tells us, the correct ironical attitude would be a most enthusiastic reaction, even a paroxysm of enthusiasm.[18] The ironist would identify himself with his interlocutor's enthusiasm, and pushing him to the extreme, would make him seem even more stupid than he is. We can give another example of the same kind. It often happens that a person insists on stating a positive fact which is actually doubtful. He might say, for example, that the table is red. The ironist would peer at him, and with a faint smile, reply: Yes indeed, the table is very, very, very red! The ironist thus affirms it while his manner suggests its denial. In the face of his "very red" the person who has insisted on the fact moderates his obstinacy and certainty, and begins to wonder if the table is all that red. The essential thing for the ironist is to have his interlocutor repudiate the immediacy of which he is aware, or rather to have him become aware of it while repudiating it. The ironist releases people from the burden imposed by the positive facts. He helps people free themselves by helping them acquire that same manner, that same power, that same factor in their life histories that he has in his own. But there is no direct impartation at all.

It should be noted that the ironist presents nothing positive to go with what he is after. The ironic reply we have analyzed neither establishes nor effectively demonstrates what the "very red" is. An attitude is called for by that remark but it is not conveyed. The red that the ironist refers to is merely a negative determination. But in the face of this exaggerated claim, the present red becomes pale, and in this way the ironic reply makes us realize that there exist several sorts of red, some of which are paler or darker than others. The ironist stretches one's conscious powers to find the qualitative differences in the phenomena and make people sensitive to them. That is why Kierkegaard considers irony, indeed, an intermediate stage between the esthetic and the ethical, but irony is also an ingredient in all mature knowing. In *Postscript*, he writes:

> Irony is a specific culture of the spirit, and therefore follows next after immediacy; then comes the ethicist, then the humorist, and finally the religious individual.[14]

The estheticist's immanental powers often lead to an obscure generality, "a mood," a single coloring of everything. The ironist's purpose is to open the eyes of the estheticist and force him to return to everyday reality and to call forth all of the qualitative differences in this world which he wishes to disregard, forget, or avoid. The ironist is too experienced in human reality to allow himself to be duped by romantic dreams. His replies make the estheticist aware of the manifold finite as such, and they do so by introducing negativity and doubt into his consciousness. The ironic reply regarding the red table may force us to recognize several kinds of red color, and it does so by referring us to that "very red" table. Like this reply, irony can also introduce negativity into consciousness in a new moral way, thus mak-

ing possible the passage from the esthetic stage of life to the ethical. The ironist, like any master of indirect communication, is a *subjective thinker*. He is a well-developed subject who is constantly striving to get free of the phenomenal world. Speaking of the subjective thinker and his indirect communication, Kierkegaard, in *Postscript* writes:

> But the genuine subjective existing thinker is always as negative as he is positive, and *vice versa*. He continues to be such as long as he exists, not once for all in a chimerical mediation. His mode of communication is made to conform, lest through being too extraordinarily communicative he should succeed in transforming a learner's existence into something different from what a human existence in general has any right to be. He is conscious of the negativity of the infinite in existence, and he constantly keeps the wound of the negative open, which in the bodily realm is sometimes the condition for a cure. The others let the wound heal over and become positive; that is to say, they are deceived. In his mode of communication he expresses the same principle. He is therefore never a teacher but a learner; and since he is always just as negative as he is positive, he is always striving.[15]

It is in order to develop and broaden his consciousness that the teacher of indirect communication, the subjective thinker, lives no longer by the immediate but finds his reality in things mediated to him by duty, by others, even by the world. This activity begins with the ironic attitude and intensifies through the ethical and religious stages. The subjective thinker lives this negativity himself, and through indirect communication he develops it in his disciple. The subjective thinker's existence—his immanence that is a synthesis of the finite and the infinite—is just as positive as it

is negative. But the positive is never completely attained. The positive synthesis always remains a "desideratum" for the unending process of appropriation. One must content himself, meanwhile, with as much negativity, the awareness of what he is not, as with the awareness of what he is.

In introducing negativity into consciousness, indirect communication transforms the person who receives it into a subject as well as a social being. In *Postscript*, Kierkegaard notes the following:

> Wherever the subjective is of importance in knowledge, and where appropriation thus constitutes the crux of the matter, the process of communication is a work of art, and doubly reflected. Its very first form is precisely the subtle principle that the personalities must be held devoutly apart from one another, and not permitted to fuse or coagulate into objectivity. It is at this point that objectivity and subjectivity part from one another.[16]

The first expression of indirect communication is, as we have seen, the verbal expression, which is a sign but is not quite what it appears to be. The thrust that this expression provokes, and the withdrawal of its objectivity that is produced in the person who pays attention to it, creates a subjective response in him. We have seen that the objective world, the world that direct communication reflects, is not qualitatively articulated. It is oddly opaqued and neither personal consciousness nor qualities can be distinguished, for everything "fuses and coagulates" in it. In introducing negativity into consciousness, indirect communication dissipates the opaqueness of objectivity. It makes consciousness withdraw from the immediately given and forces the recognition of other possibilities. Even a tree or a chair is never an accomplished given. It is by this expansion of conscious-

ness that man becomes a subject, i.e., a personal consciousness in the real sense of the word. The vast horizon and
richness of inwardness constitutes human distinction. The
richer the consciousness and the personalities of subjective
thinkers respecting even everyday objects, so the greater
the qualities and differentiations that will single out those
things from the anonymity of objectivity. On the contrary,
direct communication, such as that of the press, for instance, reduces even people to a sameness, and communicates "objective truths" of all sorts to them.

Kierkegaard's point is that richly developed personalities,
because of a richly differentiated consciousness, begin to
see and to apprehend the world in a rich variety of ways.
That is what his stages argue at some length. But this differentiation within the subject—the development of kinds
of subjectivity and kinds of consciousness—permits the
objective world to become manifest. And communication
must take these personal factors into account. On the contrary, objective communication supposes the univocal and
nonqualitative fact, which is supposedly the same for everybody. Here indifference is the order of the day, an indifferent sameness among the phenomena and indifferent temper
in the knowing subject. In fact, he, too, becomes "objective."
But at this juncture it is important to note that the very
mode of communicating supposes this indifference. Where
one can give importance to a fact, the mode of communicating matters little; but where the differentiation of the person is the aim, as in art, morals, and religion, the mode of
communication is all-important. Then indirection is requi-
site, and must be delicately fashioned so that what is required of the subject will be, while not directly stated, laid
upon the hearer or reader, nonetheless.

For an indirect communication does not permit the

relaxation of the personality. And it is only as a subject that man also can become a social being. In the anonymity of being objective, one experiences only solitude and isolation. In *Either/Or*, Kierkegaard gives a lengthy description of the solitude of the estheticist who loses himself in dreams and boredom. In fact, any abstraction, intellectual or otherwise, is a sort of isolation in which one detaches oneself from particular traits. The ironist, since he is a master of indirect communication, brings the estheticist back to the qualitative differences of everyday reality and thus helps him to become a social being. For it is only in taking note of the wealth of the finite as such that articulation is produced also in consciousness. Kierkegaard says that irony is never aimed directly at society or the public. It tends by its very nature to be the privilege of the individual.[17] The ironist, like any other master of indirect communication, teaches man to be an individual, a subject who differentiates himself from objective anonymity. And it is only as a subject that a man can establish a social life.

Kierkegaard considers Socrates a master of irony. Kierkegaard's thesis in *The Concept of Irony* aims to prove that Socrates' point of view is irony par excellence. According to Kierkegaard, Socrates has only one aim—to put the world at a distance in order to understand it. It is thus that Socrates becomes free; and his liberty, a negative one, is celebrated in the ignorance which he is constantly acknowledging. Kierkegaard writes:

> Socrates, like Samson, seizes the columns bearing the edifice of knowledge and plunges everything down into the nothingness of ignorance.[18]

By means of his irony, by making people withdraw from immediate phenomena, Socrates shows the incommensura-

bility of the phenomenon and the essence. He shakes the certainty of his interlocutors, the certainty based on those ostensibly positive facts which are actually deceptive. But on the other hand, Socrates provides no new certainty to fill the gap that is created. This is the main point of Kierkegaard's thesis on Socratic irony, and he maintains that the maieutic system does not allow people to reach any conclusions whatsoever. Analyzing the *Dialogues* of Plato, he tries to distinguish the purely Socratic attitude from the Platonic theory of ideas, which, according to him, is not attributable to Socrates. Kierkegaard maintains that Socrates does not espouse the theory of ideas and has no intention of doing so. Ideas and "essences" are for Socrates no more than negative determinations, negative ploys which find their roles in the ignorance constantly confirmed by this master of irony. It is in denying their values, in admitting himself ignorant, that Socrates expresses his relation to the *ideas*. But he does not know these ideas to be what others say they are and he does not actually possess them. Socrates is radically different. Kierkegaard writes:

> With Socrates the stream of the historical narrative plunges underground for a time like the river Guadalquivir, but only in order to burst forth again with renewed force. He functions in world history like a dash in punctuation. . . .[19]

Socrates never stops attracting people's attention, for being an ironist, "he is and he is not." He hides behind words and remains always incognito. For this reason, when we read about him, we never quite take possession of this evasive person, who constantly crosses the barrier of time that separates us from him, in order to reappear as an actual yet unknown presence. Socrates will not belong exclusively to

the past and objective history so long as one is struck by his irony. His words are always a shock, a thrust upon one's experience, and with this shock he becomes an actual presence. Of course, Socrates is also an historical person, an objective fact that has existed in the past. But in this guise Socrates is only a possible that exists in consciousness, a possible among others that are learned directly from historical accounts. His irony actualizes him as a person for the qualified reader. The truth is that anybody may be an historical or a transhistorical other, depending on the form of his communication. As a conglomeration of objective phenomena, any other person is only an historical other for me. I see, for instance, that he is moving before me, that he is doing something. But the conglomeration of phenomena is only a possible existing in me; only an artistic communication or thrust makes him otherwise. He then becomes almost transhistorical whether I like it or not, and this confrontation differs from the kind I have with ordinary things. Beyond the words I read, Socrates himself is always there as an actual presence that provokes a shock. But it is the ironic style, not just the words, which does that.

We have now studied the observations of Kierkegaard on irony as indirect communication and on Socrates as a master of irony. Whether or not Kierkegaard is correct in every detail in so presenting the Socratic attitude is of secondary importance. (As a matter of fact, Kierkegaard is too much influenced by the picture of Socrates given by Aristophanes.) What is important is the way in which Kierkegaard interprets Socratic thought. We shall see later that Kierkegaard's philosophy is likewise indirect communication; it is slightly mocking and has an air of contradictoriness about it which disengages the reader from the immediate content. Because man tends to believe that he possesses that content, because he often identifies himself with the immediate, he

does not even suspect that he is actually in a state of ignorance. We shall see in chapter nine that the question posed by Kierkegaard is not how truth can be learned, but how error or ignorance is learned. In Kierkegaard's opinion, the maieutic system constitutes an answer to this question, and all indirect communication is such a system.

Like irony, humor is also an indirect communication. It too is the union of jest and earnest, and it differs from irony only in that its meaning is deeper. In *The Concept of Irony*, Kierkegaard deals with the two together,[20] but he notes the more serious nature of humor and explains it more clearly in *Postscript*. Irony is in general contemptuous, even aggressive, while humor has a touch of gentleness, affectionate good nature, and humility. Humor is often indicative of mature, deep, and quasi-religious inwardness, and Kierkegaard considers it an intermediate stage between the ethical and the religious. The humorist knows the precariousness and finiteness of the human condition, and in reflecting upon it he relaxes in jest. But even if he is not a believer, his communication already evinces a latent despair. Nothing in the present life seems stable or valid to him, and he constantly renounces the immediate. His communication shocks the people around him, though more gently than that of the ironist, to be sure. Like the ironist, however, the humorist makes people withdraw from the immediate while he remains incognito behind his communication. One does not know what he thinks. Feeling guilty, he practices humility and resignation in his life, and his replies can take people to the threshold of the religious stage.

Now that we have seen Kierkegaard's observations on irony and humor, we shall look into his reflections on the art of literature. Kierkegaard maintains that literary artfulness must be indirect communication, too. In the *Journals* he writes:

Chapter 7

The law of delicacy by which an author is permitted to use what he has himself experienced is that he never says the truth but keeps the truth for himself and only lets it emerge in different ways.[21]

In this passage Kierkegaard formulates the rule which should, in his opinion, govern all literary work; and though he speaks only of literary work, it is perhaps true that this law could be generalized to cover all artistic production. A work of art cannot be the direct statement of some truth, nor a simple copy of nature, nor an historical account of events. Let us consider the following passage, taken from *The Present Age*:

What is *talkativeness*? It is the result of doing away with the vital distinction between talking and keeping silent. Only some one who knows how to remain essentially silent can really talk—and act essentially. Silence is the essence of inwardness, of the inner life. . . . The law governing artistic production applies, on a smaller scale, to every one in daily life. Every man who has a real experience experiences at the same time all its possibilities in an ideal sense, including the opposite possibility. Esthetically these possibilities are his lawful property. Not so, however, his private and personal reality. His talk and his production both rest upon his silence. The ideal perfection of his talk and of his production will correspond to his silence, and the absolute expression of that silence will be that the ideal will include the qualitatively opposite possibility. But as soon as the artist prostitutes his own reality he is no longer essentially productive. His beginning is his end, and his very first word will be a sin against the modesty of the ideal. This type of artistic production is therefore even, esthetically speaking, a kind of

private gossip. It is easily recognized because it is not balanced by its opposite; for ideality is the balance of opposites. For example, if the man who is moved to write by suffering is really initiated into the realm of ideals, he will reproduce the happiness as well as the suffering of his experiences with the same affection. The condition of his attaining this ideal is the silence with which he shuts off his own real personality. Otherwise, in spite of all precautions, such as changing the scene to Africa, his one-sided predilection will be privately recognizable. For an author, like any one else, must have his own private personality, but it must be his own Holy of Holies;* and just as the entrance to a house is barred by the crossed bayonets of the guards, the approach to a man's personality is barred by the dialectical cross of qualitative opposites in an ideal equilibrium.[22]

In the inward reflection of the subjective thinker, the positive is often expressed by the negative. It is through unhappiness experienced at present that happiness is glimpsed. Ethical perfection and eternal happiness find their expression in repentance and guilt feelings. The subjective thinker never has a one-dimensional and unequivocal experience that he can sum up for others in a direct formulation. That is why he likes silence. The given character of language is unable to express his inwardness—the expression must be extralinguistic and part of "how" it is said, not "what" is said. For a trivial consciousness, happiness, for instance, becomes an objective fact that is felt and recognized by signs that are no less objective (money, social position, etc.). Since it is caught up in objective facts, the alienated consciousness lends itself to the positive and direct discourse offered by objective accounts and chitchat. Thus it

* Author's note: In the text it is written in Greek.

states itself by saying: I am happy. I am satisfied, etc. It places a period after each statement for the purpose of assuring us that we are dealing with a well-founded positive fact. But positivity and objectivity are thus merely the prostitution of inwardness. An objective fact, since it is an arbitrary fixation, or an abstraction that disregards personal traits, can actually belong to everybody. The more this fact pretends to be positive, the more it becomes the property of the public, and this passage from subjectivity to objectivity is in fact a prostitution of inwardness. A writer, or any man, who directly displays his inwardness is only prostituting his inward reality, says Kierkegaard.

Any profound experience, since it is never unequivocal, can be expressed only by indirect communication, which, according to Kierkegaard, requires an "artistic communication," full of secrets.[23] The subjective thinker must let his truth emerge in different ways, for that is the way he experiences it himself. Since he has a dialectical power, any ideal that he aspires to must have a relation to his actual and finite reality. The subjective thinker always achieves an ideality by giving up something, and it is through giving up that he forges his ideal concepts concerning happiness, luck, fortune, and the rest. But the finite events experienced never have an unambiguous meaning. Let us recall Constantius, the pseudonymous author of *Repetition*, who compares life with a spectacle "which no one calls a comedy, no one a tragedy, because no one knows the end." In view of the ambiguous meanings of finite events, the ideals which the subjective thinker extracts from them are also equivocal. That is why his artistic communication will disclose happiness as well as unhappiness with the same detachment, for instance. Encountering the romantic art criticized by Kierkegaard, which worships abstract and often hypos-

tatized ideas, the artistic communication of the subjective thinker cannot evoke a fixed and positive ideal which would provide an infallible panacea for human well-being. Being conscious of the relativity which rules life, this thinker practices humility in his own life as well as in his communications. That is why the ideality that he expresses is modestly and conjecturally presented. His life gives evidence of happiness as well as unhappiness, and he himself evinces as much restraint in laughing as in crying; and even tears and laughter have their duplicity. The inner life of the subjective thinker has as much comedy in it as pathos; it is a mixture of the comic and the tragic.[24]

We now understand Kierkegaard's opinion that a balance of opposites must obtain when any profound ideality is being advanced. Let us note also that the equilibrium does not reduce to a state of rest or a nothing in which logical contradictions annul each other. What we have here is a dialectical relationship between qualitative contraries manifested through each other, and it is indirect communication which allows these qualitative opposites to root themselves in the person who receives them. A work of art, in which opposite possibilities of human reality are presented, is itself a sign of contradiction which makes people pull back from their fixed ideas and prejudices. For example, a work of art expressing happiness and unhappiness seen through each other might very well impel people to redefine what they mean by happiness and unhappiness. Indirect communication does not produce a state of repose in the soul of the person receiving it. On the contrary, it develops a tension that encourages people to a personal secretiveness and inwardness of which they have heretofore been ignorant, since they have been too attached to the obvious aspects of things.

8.

Consciousness and Indirect Communication

A YEAR after Kierkegaard's death, a novel was published in France which is a perfect example, to my mind, of the law of artistic production that Kierkegaard talks about. The novel is Flaubert's *Madame Bovary*. The character "Madame Bovary" is not an historical fact nor did Flaubert intend to provide us with an historical account. In fact, we cannot be sure if the character is meant to be a woman or a man—Flaubert himself. Emma Bovary is a concept which contains its own opposite, without at the same time losing touch with everyday, concrete reality. The reader sees Emma Bovary rise to great heights of sensibility despite the stifling pettiness of small-town life, and cannot help but be attracted to her in her struggle to overcome the banality and materialism of everyday life, which is so often tainted by piosity. At the same time, however, the reader cannot overlook Emma Bovary's affectations and lack of discipline, her lies and whims, all of which make her an incarnation of self-centeredness. On the other hand, Madame Bovary is sometimes forced to lying and whim, without actually wishing either. She frequently falls victim to the vicious circles spun round her by circumstances of life. As a figment, then, Emma Bovary is at one and the same time the embodiment of elevated piety and repulsive selfishness. This dialectic is constantly visible in reality, the very reality of which

128

Madame Bovary is half victim and half accomplice. It is for this reason that we cannot sit in judgment upon her. On the contrary, we feel pity for her, recommending her to the mercy of God. At the end of the novel, Flaubert describes the corpse of Emma Bovary as it has been dressed for the wake. "She's still attractive," says the innkeeper's wife. Flaubert uses this contrast between life and death to make us reflect on what a mortal creature can do in this world. Flaubert's novel asks some questions without answering them. It makes us turn inwards to reflect upon and discover ourselves.

Flaubert, also, is worthy of being considered a master of indirect communication because he does not intrude himself into the development of the novel nor take any part in it. He himself is simply an objective witness, and his own inwardness remains incognito. It required a trial to determine the real intentions of Flaubert, just as it required one to judge the proposals of Socrates. But the inwardness of Flaubert, or Socrates, or any master of indirect communication will always be a secret, a secret object that one tries to take possession of, to no avail. And like the inwardness of Flaubert or Socrates, that of Kierkegaard is also a secret, for the philosophy of Kierkegaard is an indirect communication which hides his inwardness from us.

The aim of Kierkegaard's philosophy is to convert people to the religious life. Christianity requires man to struggle constantly against the immediate, for only the total renunciation of the finite prepares man for the religious leap by the help of which the existence of the Absolute will be revealed to him. Now Kierkegaard as master of indirect communication wants to help people free themselves of the immediate. In order to do this, he does not teach Christianity directly, nor does he specifically ask the reader to re-

nounce his immediate life and believe in God. Quite the contrary. In order to open the eyes of the esthetic reader, Kierkegaard assumes the guise of a romantic writer. But like the ironist, he affirms the phenomenon while denying it. He pretends to be an estheticist, totally enchanted by romantic ideas, but at the same time he shows up the emptiness of the esthetic life. For Kierkegaard does not fail to present the other aspects of esthetic life, such as melancholy, boredom, and despair. The esthetic reality which Kierkegaard depicts is like a sign of contradiction, a union of qualitative opposites, which draws the reader away from the esthetic life by making him understand that there is nothing permanent or reassuring in it. It is essential, however, that the reader discover this truth for himself, and Kierkegaard does not wish to communicate it directly. It is the reader himself who must understand that the esthetic life is merely one existential possibility among many. That is why Kierkegaard always presents several existential possibilities in his works. Esthetic, ethical, demoniacal, and religious characters confront each other in the same volume, and it is through the confrontation of qualitatively opposite possibilities that the reader learns to know the *possible* as such. Like every other method of indirect communication, Kierkegaard's philosophy lures us into the area of the possible; it is a seduction which ends with the discovery of the possible itself, of the possible *qua* possible. The reader comes to learn that his own immanence contains nothing but possibles, and in this *negative* manner he experiences transcendent existence. In order to see this point more clearly, let us return to the questions posed at the beginning of chapter seven.

The first question concerned transcendent existence. We have seen, in dealing with this question, that nothing can be

stated about a truly unknown thing, nor can this thing even be said to exist. "Existence" is not a meaningful predicate. The second question raised the problem of solipsism, and we wondered whether Kierkegaard's philosophy is not itself solipsistic. The two questions resolve into one, since we are dealing with that which exists *outside* of consciousness. Now if philosophical contemplation cannot attain existence, if it is impossible to know that which is outside of a thought, the philosopher, too, must give up contemplation and resort to action. Recognizing the impossibility of attaining transcendent existence by means of thought, Kierkegaard replaces philosophical contemplation with a kind of philosophical activity. The first lines of *Repetition* will explain what we mean by a philosophical activity:

> When the Eleatic School denied the possibility of motion, Diogenes, as everybody knows, stepped forth as an opponent. He *stepped* forth literally, for he said not a word, but merely walked several times back and forth, thinking that thereby he had sufficiently refuted those philosophers.[1]

Where thought fails, activity may still be resorted to. Like Diogenes, Kierkegaard takes recourse in activity so that people may understand things that are inaccessible to thought. He deals with existence, and makes us understand that it exists without saying a word about it. Indirect communication is precisely that activity that makes us experience existence as an object of passion. In the *Journals*, Kierkegaard stresses the fact that all indirect communication is "a communication of capability (Kunnens Meddelelse)" and not "a communication of knowledge (Videns Meddelelse)," which is direct communication.[2] Indirect communication conveys nothing positive, since it is a sign of contradiction

whose aim is precisely to make people draw away from positive facts.[3] Indirect communication is a shock that pushes people away from the phenomena and thus constrains them to keep their distance. It increases human capacity. The distance itself acquaints people with the fact that the phenomena are no more than possibles. Thrown into the void, and thus experiencing the flight of phenomena provoked by the sign of contradiction, man realizes that the phenomena are only possibles. At this moment he becomes aware of the error and ignorance in which he has lived up to then, believing wrongly that the possible is the real and that immanental life is the only one that matters. The shock provoked by indirect communication reveals the possible as such to man, and this is then the negative way of experiencing transcendent existence or the outside world. We have said that through the shock, one "experiences" transcendent existence and not that one "knows" it, for experiencing concerns an activity, a compulsion that is felt. Only in faith can one positively attain transcendent existence, or, as Kierkegaard says, "the second immediacy." But faith is conditioned by the prerequisite attitude of resignation. In order to become a Christian, one must first of all take leave of the familiar by resignation, in order to take a good look at it and get to know its nature. It is only a master of indirect communication who makes people maintain this distance. Such a teacher makes no statement concerning existence or the difference between it and the appearance of things. But he makes us experience the force of existence by his manner of speech and behavior. He attacks us while withdrawing incognito, and his communication produces the movement of becoming in us even while the positive exercises itself through the negative. By means of the shock which he provokes, we experience his own actual presence

outside ourselves, and thus we are helped to avoid a solipsism. Every direct communication only affirms a solipsism,
and indirect communication alone leads us outside what is
said to be reality.

Aware of the fact that nothing can be stated directly concerning transcendence, Kierkegaard speaks to the reader
through this subtle philosophical activity. That activity, as
it were, accompanies what is said. His philosophical production is an indirect communication and, in fact, the
purely philosophical part of this production is within that
form in which it is couched for his readers. This explains,
too, Kierkegaard's decision to make use of pseudonyms in
his literary activity. In "A First and Last Declaration" at
the end of *Postscript*, Kierkegaard includes the following
statement which is important to study:

> My pseudonymity or polynymity has not had a *casual*
> [my italics] ground in my *person* . . . but it has an *essen-
> tial* ground in the character of the *production*. . . . What
> is written therefore is in fact mine, but only in so far as
> I put into the mouth of the poetically actual individuality
> whom I *produced*, his life-view expressed in audible
> lines. For my relation is even more external than that of
> a poet, who poetizes characters, and yet in the preface is
> himself the author. For I am impersonal, or am personal
> in the [third] person,* a *souffleur* who has poetically pro-
> duced the *authors*, whose preface in turn is their own
> production, as are even their own names. So in the pseu-
> donymous works there is not a single word which is mine,
> I have no opinion about these works except as *third per-
> son* [my italics], no knowledge of their meaning except
> as a reader, not the remotest private relation to them,

* Author's note: The English edition mistakenly reads "second
person."

since such a thing is impossible in the case of a doubly reflected communication. One single word of mine uttered
personally in my own name would be an instance of pre-
sumptuous self-forgetfulness, and dialectically viewed it
would incur with one word the guilt of annihilating the
pseudonyms.[4]

Pseudonymity, an essential element in the production of
Kierkegaard, is a doubly-reflected indirect communication.
Kierkegaard subsequently emphasizes that he does not
want to identify himself with the characters created by him,
the more so because some of them are esthetic characters.
Like all masters of indirect communication, he is an objective witness of his own production. In his works he communicates to us existential possibilities that are qualitatively
opposite, and he does so while withdrawing and hiding behind his pseudonyms. The existence of Kierkegaard acti-
vates us while retiring from us, and it thus releases reflection in us. We reflect on the words of Kierkegaard, we ask
ourselves questions, etc. The reflection makes a multiplicity
of factors emerge in consciousness, and thus broadens its
horizon. But in this flux of emerging phenomena, the real
existence of the master of indirect communication does not
actually intrude. Nothing said or done as such are ever
proof of Kierkegaard, the existing subject. The person who
receives the indirect communication experiences the shock
that it provokes, but he does not know the agent who is the
source of it and who is outside of himself. The existence of
Kierkegaard is not located in his works, and the pseudonyms he used are a clear expression of this absence. Instead,
it is the very distance of the author's existence which forces
one to worry about his own existence. One has to become
something himself even while the existence of Kierkegaard

is hidden. But staying hidden is the real art and task of indirect communication.

We have seen that each particular phenomenal occurrence means the negation and distancing of real existence. Every conscious activity is always the banishment of being *qua* being. Even if I say "I," this "I" is not the existence, which has already moved away. In saying "I," I make myself foreign to myself and to my own transcendent existence. Being an "I" is not a conceptual experience. It is not I that have expressed the "I"; it is someone else, a stranger. The grammatical subject and the real subject are strangers to one another. The phenomenal domain never proves an *existing* subject. The only subject found in it is the one that the use of language requires. But this subject is "anyone," since in any case it is a matter of an arbitrary fixation created by language. "I" belongs to everybody in turn. Language fixes phenomena in concepts or names, thus creating the subjects "table," "tree," "David," "Jean," etc. But these subjects do not have the same existence in the phenomenal and linguistic domain as they do in actual existence. Actually, the word "I" could be eliminated from the language, and "he" could be used in referring to oneself, for the subject of language is always the third person. As to Kierkegaard, instead of avoiding the word "I," he prefers to do what amounts to the same thing—use pseudonyms in his writing. It is not Kierkegaard who speaks through his writings, it is, as he says, a "third person," a "prompter," in short, a "someone" who is the pseudonym. This again is the philosophical activity that consists of communicating so that the writing subject retreats incognito thus forcing the reader to become the true subject, not on paper or in concepts, but in existence.

Kierkegaard makes his pseudonymous authors undertake

the same action that he himself undertook several times in writing his works. Hidden behind the pseudonym Victor Eremita, he published *Either/Or*. But Eremita is not presented as the author of the work; he is only the publisher. Victor Eremita tells us that the book was written by two authors, A and B. In other words, they, too, are unknown authors. Author A supposedly wrote the first part, which includes *The Diary of the Seducer*. But Victor Eremita, in the preface, emphasizes that Author A is not the author of the *Diary* but only its publisher. In *Repetition*, the pseudonymous author Constantin Constantius presents the character of the young man to us, and in doing so, also retreats. On the last page of the book, he tells us that he himself is a "forsvindende" person, i.e., a transitory figure who disappears "like a midwife in relation to the child she has brought to birth." The pseudonymous author of *Stages on Life's Way* likewise vanishes. Hilarius says that he is not the author, but only the binder of a book written by a person long dead. The book has several characters, one of which, Brother Taciturnus, editorializes about the diary, "Guilty/ Not Guilty," while telling us that he found it in a lake. He even requests the reader to try to find out who the author is.

The fact that this phenomenal linguistic domain does not tell us about being *qua* being, and that one is therefore forced to address even oneself via the third person, is also expressed indirectly in the following manner. Kierkegaard does not introduce a single person in his works who says directly: "I am a believer, a Christian." To speak in this way would be to utter nonsense. Faith does not allow itself to be testified to by words alone, for it requires not just words but a leap, which leads man beyond immanence and words, that he may attain his transcendent existence, his real ego.

Now this ego cannot describe itself as Christian. The moment one thinks of this ego, one is no longer Christian. When one wants to speak of faith, it stops being a positive reality and becomes a possibility. Thus for Johannes Climacus, the pseudonymous author of *Postscript* and *Philosophical Fragments*, Christianity is but a possibility, and he himself is, as he says, only a humorist. Kierkegaard knows very well that one cannot speak of the true qualities of one's life nor of one's own faith. This is not the form they demand. That is why his works always have two characters, one of which describes the other as a believer. In *Fear and Trembling*, Johannes de Silentio tells us that Abraham is a believer, and stresses that Abraham himself does not speak. In *Repetition*, Constantius tells us that the young man has a religious "sentiment," and the young man in turn says that Job is a believer who has experienced repetition in his faith. In *Stages on Life's Way*, Brother Taciturnus says that "Quidam," i.e., the unknown author of the diary, "Guilty/Not Guilty," is "a demoniacal character in the direction of the religious." And finally, Kierkegaard doubts whether he himself is a Christian and uses Anti-Climacus, the pseudonymous character in *The Sickness unto Death* and *Training in Christianity* as the model of the real Christian.[5] However, Anti-Climacus speaks not of himself, but of Jesus. It is therefore always someone else who says that another is a believer. As to the words of Jesus, they are not ordinary words, but words which are already performances. We shall see that according to Kierkegaard, Christianity is not doctrine but life. Though faith can use ordinary and direct words, it is not the case that words are the faith—they are at best only about it. Faith is more than words.

Kierkegaard did not use pseudonyms in publishing his *Edifying Discourses* because he wanted to show that he was

a religious writer even though he had published esthetical works. But the discourses do not deal with faith except as an immanental possibility, and in *Postscript* Kierkegaard says that they belong to immanental religiousness which is not Christianity.[6] During 1843 and 1844 Kierkegaard published eighteen discourses whose prefaces are noteworthy. He stresses that he does not aim to teach anything objective.[7] The discourses are edifying discourses and not doctrine. They are a sort of exercise leading to the realization of the religious life. Kierkegaard adds by the way that while giving his discourses to readers, he would still like to be "botreist," i.e., a person who is gone and no longer present.[8] In another preface, Kierkegaard hopes that his readers will forget him,[9] and in still another, he says that he is turning to his readers only to "tage afsked," i.e., to take leave of them.[10] Kierkegaard wants to be incognito at the same time that he publishes those heartfelt pieces under his own name. He is always the master of indirect communication who withdraws while communicating.

We have just studied the essence of Kierkegaard's philosophy. This philosophy is not a conceptual exercise only, but is rather a philosophical activity. We have seen that the main principle of Kierkegaard's philosophy concerns the chasm which separates the possible—the phenomenon—from the being *qua* being. Now this principle is ineffable and states a limit from the philosophical point of view, for any pronouncement on it would be unjustifiable. But where philosophical reflection fails, philosophical activity takes over. Kierkegaard's pseudonymity, this literary hide-and-seek which seems so astonishing and incomprehensible, is in fact part of this philosophical activity. Kierkegaard communicates qualitatively opposite existential possibilities and hides himself at the same time. In the course of this literary

hide-and-seek, he draws his readers into considering various possibilities, until they discover the one for themselves and thus move outside of the possibility into a new kind of existence. Readers constantly seek the inwardness and existence of Kierkegaard instead, but Kierkegaard is always absent; and his works shock one into a new form of life by oneself. Kierkegaard makes us withdraw from what we are so that we may discover a new possible for ourselves. In this way Kierkegaard leads his readers toward the religious life, where the transcendent is revealed. The essence of Kierkegaard's philosophy is not in what he says directly, but in the form of communication which elicits and is an activity, an indirect communication that gives one a new capability.

It is true that Kierkegaard also states his philosophical principle in other forms. He emphasizes many times, in *Postscript* and elsewhere, that thought and being are not identical. He also speaks directly of God and the existence of Jesus. But these pronouncements have only a suggestive value, and no philosophical validity. From the philosophical point of view, nothing can be stated regarding existence, since one does not know it. That is why Kierkegaard, who is well aware of this philosophical impossibility, has Johannes Climacus, the pseudonymous author of *Postscript*, say the following at the end of the book:

> So then the book is superfluous; let no one therefore take the pains to appeal to it as an authority; for he who thus appeals to it has *eo ipso* misunderstood it. . . . so what I write contains also a piece of information to the effect that everything is so to be understood that it is understood to be revoked, and the book has not only a Conclusion but a Revocation.[11]

Kierkegaard asks us not to consider *Postscript* to be au-

thoritative. This book, in which Kierkegaard deals with existence as well as Christianity directly, is but superfluous. That is an admission on the part of Kierkegaard that the work has no permanent validity. It is as if he said: "As a philosopher, I can state nothing about existence. I have done so, however, but this has only a suggestive value and I retract it." The existence spoken of is merely a possible, and the faith presented is only a possibility. Johannes Climacus tells us that he himself is only a humorist who makes experiments. Let us note also that the chapter that is perhaps the most important one in *Philosophical Fragments* is called "A Project of Thought." In this chapter, Kierkegaard speaks of the encounter between God and man in the moment of faith. We shall come back to what Kierkegaard says in that chapter, for it deals with the relationship between transcendence and man. What interests us at the moment is the fact that the chapter is entitled as it is. Everything real and actual in the moment of faith is, to an author, only a project of thought, i.e., a hypothetical possibility. The philosopher cannot formulate the ineffable in words, and Kierkegaard does not consider his propositions on this score to be philosophical results. He tells us that his words only make a hypothesis, and that they only allude and cannot make the fundamental difference that faith itself does. But this, too, is an indirect communication, for to say something and thus to recant is to communicate, albeit under a kind of contradictory bit of language.

Having studied the form of Kierkegaard's literary production, we shall, along with Kierkegaard, recapitulate the essential characteristics of indirect communication.

Indirect communication forces the person who receives it to a kind of movement away from immediate phenomena. Kierkegaard wishes to lead his readers to Christianity. But

as a philosopher, he cannot make faith germinate in a man. He can only invite him, tease him into the renunciation of what he is, and show him that the immediate is only a possible. But as people are generally recalcitrant about this renunciation, Kierkegaard intends to force the awareness of it upon them. In *The Point of View on My Work as An Author*, Kierkegaard writes the following:

> That even if a man will not follow where one endeavors to lead him, one thing it is still possible to do for him— compel him to take notice.[12]

Every indirect communication says something but it also does something. It is like an arrow thrust into the person who receives it. One suffers its presence. One cannot avoid the cutting remarks of the ironist, nor the effect of humor. The master of indirect communication forces us to renounce our ideas and our prejudices, but more, too—even our way of life, everything that previously had seemed objective and unshakable. We are forced to be attentive to new possibilities as such. This is the negative and indirect way of experiencing what is outside of ourselves and thus comprehending the limits of what we are. Though the ironist, for instance, is not a Christian, he takes people along the path that leads to Christianity.

The constraint that indirect communication places upon us only helps us to become free. Indirect communication communicates little that is objective, and its aim actually is to pry people loose from objective burdens. It reminds people of their error and ignorance, and consequently they begin seeking something new for themselves. Indirect communication forces people to free themselves, for it produces in them the resignation and the coming-out-of-oneself which are the essence of freedom.[13] And it is by learning to

141

come out of himself, and becoming aware of the possible as such, that man prepares for the religious coming-out-of-himself which takes him toward transcendence. In order to free himself finally from all immediacy, man needs the constraint of the transhistorical other. But this constraint is like the aid of a midwife who forces the woman whose child is being delivered to relax. Every master of indirect communication forces people to relax and free themselves of objective burdens. Let us remember, however, that the constraint applied by indirect communication does not resemble physical constraint. It is rather a sort of artistic persuasion, for all indirect communication is an art.

In *The Point of View*, Kierkegaard considers indirect communication even a sort of deceit of which his own esthetic production is an example. He writes:

> What then does it mean, "to deceive"? It means that one does not begin *directly* with the matter one wants to communicate, but begins by accepting the other man's illusion as good money. So (to stick to the theme with which this work especially deals) one does not begin thus: I am a Christian; you are not a Christian. Nor does one begin thus: It is Christianity I am proclaiming; and you are living in purely esthetic categories. No, one begins thus: Let us talk about esthetics. The deception consists in the fact that one talks thus merely to get to the religious theme. But, on our assumption, the other man is under the illusion that the esthetic is Christianity; for, he thinks, I am a Christian, and yet he lives in esthetic categories.[14]

The master of indirect communication deceives people by pretending to be in agreement with their ideas, even with their illusions. But despite his master's approval, the disciple suddenly finds himself emptied of his own ideas and

torn away from his convictions. This is a device of indirect communication, for it affirms one thing while demanding its contrary. The constraint that indirect communication exercises is thus deceitful, for it is a seductive constraint, whose aim, says Kierkegaard, is to lead the disciple to the truth.[15] Of course, this communication does not in itself communicate the truth. What it does is provoke the disciple to inner reflection, and the disciple, now aware of his error, renounces it and seeks truth. Indirect communication introduces negativity into consciousness and actually teaches people about their lives. During this internal contemplation, each possibility is seen through its qualitative contrary, and the more the dialectical contemplation is intensified, the more poignant one's consciousness becomes. In *Postscript*, Kierkegaard writes:

> To abstract from existence is to remove the difficulty. To remain in existence so as to understand one thing in one moment and another thing in another moment, is not to understand oneself. But to understand the greatest oppositions together, and to understand oneself existing in them, is very difficult. Let anyone merely observe himself, and take note of how men speak, and he will perceive how rarely this task is successfully realized.[16]

Certainly, it is difficult to always live this dialectical union of qualitative opposites. One is quickly exhausted by viewing this vast horizon offered by dialectical reflection, where all aspects of things are simultaneously displayed. One is especially exhausted by the renunciation of the finite and the constant recognition of one's futility in the face of infinity. Through laziness or pride one often tends to sum up inward experience, break down one's life into little "objective" pieces, and as a result one understands "one thing

in one moment and another thing in another moment." It is precisely the impetus provided by indirect communication which makes one consciously negative towards oneself and forces one to a new kind of subjectivity and social being.

In *Works of Love*, Kierkegaard wonders: "Which is more difficult, to awaken one who sleeps, or to awaken one who, awake, dreams that he is awake?"[17] Of course most people are not really awake. They only dream that they are, but actually their open eyes see nothing. The greater part of our lives is lived in alienation, where our consciousness is out of joint. We have adopted a system of values which we believe are objective and true but which give us no satisfaction. One way or another human consciousness always knows enough objective facts; man always knows something. But he does not know that he is actually in error, and that his immediate knowledge is only a single possibility among others. Thus no man is at rest—he is alienated from his goal and happiness. Kierkegaard is interested in the question of apprenticing oneself, as did Socrates, to ignorance, and his theory of indirect communication is the reply. This communication, being a maieutic system reminding people of their error, is the only thing that can make us come out of our solipsism and alienation. The teacher who thus communicates resembles the angels who made Lot leave Sodom, thereby helping him to repudiate the life he had led in that town. Once he was outside the town, Lot was open to the new things he was about to encounter. Like the angels, the teacher of indirect communication spurs his learners from the immediacies which surround them toward new and unheard of possibilities manifested by God.

9.

The Christian Consciousness and the Problem of Truth

In the *Journals*, Kierkegaard declares:

> They can do whatever they want with me now, insult me, envy me, disparage my books, attack me, kill me; they will never in all eternity be able to dispute—which was my idea, the basis of my life—that one of the most original ideas in many centuries, and the most original ever expressed in Danish, is that Christianity needed an expert in maieutics, and that I was the one, while nobody appreciated this. This category for deploying Christianity does not suit Christendom. Here it is maieutics which is suitable, for it takes as its point of departure the notion that people have the highest good, but wishes to help them realize what they have.[1]

Kierkegaard believes that he is an expert in maieutics and we now understand the task that he has undertaken. Instead of teaching Christianity directly, Kierkegaard restricts himself to making his readers understand that they are in error. He reproaches the established order (Christendom) with having transformed Christianity into an objective doctrine that is taught directly. But it should be noted that Kierkegaard's philosophical production, aside from the fact that it is a maieutic communication, aims to show that Christianity itself is likewise indirect communication in

which Jesus is the teacher. In order to study this point, let us return to Kierkegaard's reflection on religiousness A and B.

Through resignation and through his feelings of guilt, the believer of the A type of religiousness aspires to eternal blessedness and to God. But as his inward reflection is primarily self-negating, eternal blessedness, God, and the sovereign good for which he strives are no more than negative determinations for him. It is in becoming aware of the limits of his human condition that the believer of religiousness A begins to yearn for and believe in God. But for him, God is scarcely more than an object, to be approximated by endless effort, starting with the process of negation where he is constantly renouncing the finite and human world. In this reflective stance of the believer, God is merely a negative determination and not yet a real component in one's existence. That is why religiousness A is not, according to Kierkegaard, pronouncedly Christian, though it requires, as does Christianity, the renunciation of the finite world. Religiousness of this type could even be pagan, for it lacks the essential confidence of Christianity—that God, as a real and transcendent existence, has appeared in time. That God should have appeared at one time, that God should have actually become a particular and transcendent existence, this is the incomprehensible part, the absolute paradox which only Christian faith can accept:

> Immanently (in the fantastic medium of abstraction) God does not *exist*, he only is—God only exists for an existing man, i.e., he can only exist in *faith*. Providence, atonement, etc., only exist for an existing man. . . . Faith is therefore the anticipation of the eternal which holds the factors together, the cleavages of existence. When an

existing individual does not have faith, God *is* not, neither does God *exist*, although understood from an eternal point of view God is eternally.[2]

Faith is the anticipation of the eternal which holds the factors and cleavages of existence together. Only through faith can one cross the barriers, otherwise insurmountable, between the negativity of resigning the finite and the positivity of embracing the infinite being. God as real existence exists only for faith; in other words, God does not obtrude upon reflection, He only *is*, like any other possible, in an immanental way. Kierkegaard considers the moment (Øjeblikket) of faith to be the moment of man's rebirth. At that moment, the believer brings himself to birth, acquires his own existence, his own ego, while being face to face with Christ.

But Christian faith is conditioned by religiousness A. Religiousness B can be attained only in the presence of the prerequisite which consists of renouncing the finite. In order to become a Christian, man needs training in this movement of resignation or in what Kierkegaard calls "the immense detour of dying from immediacy." Indirect communication must therefore intensify religiousness A as much as possible, until it becomes a total abnegation which is expressed in Christian love. Because it is very difficult to be constantly fighting the immediate and because it is even more painful to learn to renounce self-esteem, man needs a teacher to help him "die from immediacy." Certainly the ironist, the humorist, and Socrates himself contribute a great deal to this end, for they teach people to draw back and gain detachment. Being human beings, they cannot, however, produce total self-abnegation in the learners. No human being can serve as an impetus for the love evinced

147

by Christianity. Only Jesus, the God-Man, can do this, and indeed He does. God decided to become a man in order to teach people to love, and as a paradigm of this love Jesus is, according to Kierkegaard, the teacher of an indirect communication which has as its first aim the self-abnegation of a man. Of course, this is only the wound before the cure, but it is the necessary wound.

In dealing with the subject of Christianity, Kierkegaard remains faithful to his conceptual delineations. As a philosopher, he can state nothing conceptual about God, for he does not *know* transcendence in a conceptual and intellective way. What the philosopher knows is Jesus as a man, i.e., Jesus as a phenomenon. In *Training in Christianity*, Kierkegaard analyzes the invitation of Jesus: "Come hither unto me, all ye that labour and are heavy laden, I will give you rest." Kierkegaard asks:

> The Inviter. Who is the Inviter? Jesus Christ. Which Jesus Christ? The Jesus Christ who sits in glory at the right hand of the Father? No. From the seat of His glory He has not spoken one word. Therefore it is Jesus Christ in His humiliation, in the state of humiliation, who spoke these words.

> Is then Jesus Christ not always the same? Yes, He is the same yesterday and today, the same that 1,800 years ago humbled Himself and took upon Him the form of a servant, the Jesus Christ who uttered these words of invitation. In His coming again in glory He is again the same Jesus Christ; but this has not yet occurred.[3]

For every man, philosopher included, Jesus looks first of all like another man, a human phenomenon described in the New Testament. But it is in dealing with this human being who is said to be God that Kierkegaard formulates ever

more precisely his ideas on Christianity as an indirect communication. In *Training of Christianity*, Kierkegaard recalls that the God-Man is also called a sign of contradiction in the scriptures (Luke 2:34). He explains the meaning of the term "sign" in this connection, and notes, as we have seen, that the unity of jest and earnest is also an example of a sign of contradiction.[4] So Jesus, says Kierkegaard, is not a simple phenomenon, but rather a contradictory one. Just as in the case of profound humor, Jesus is a sign disguising contrarieties in its composition. Kierkegaard writes:

> When one says directly, "I am God; the Father and I are one," that is direct communication. But when he who says it is an individual man, quite like other men, then this communication is not just perfectly direct; for it is not just perfectly clear and direct that an individual man should be God—although what he says is perfectly direct. By reason of the communicator the communication contains a contradiction, it becomes indirect communication, it puts to thee a choice, whether thou wilt believe Him or not.[5]

Jesus is a contradictory unity. On the one hand, He is a man "born of a despised maiden, His father a carpenter,"[6] the man who is "betrayed, mocked, spit upon, scourged."[7] In the believer's eyes, Jesus represents everything lowly in the world; He is lowliness itself. But on the other hand, and this is the incomprehensible paradox, this man says that He is God. While He is insulted and shamed, He gives evidence of devotion and sacrifice such as no other human being. Jesus suffers and allows Himself to be crucified for the sake of His persecutors, all of whom He loves. He Himself is thus a synthesis of incommensurables, the lowly and the sublime, godliness and manliness.

Chapter 9

Kierkegaard emphasizes, in *Training in Christianity*, that
the persecution of Jesus is by no means a coincidence to be
explained by accidental circumstances of his life. Quite the
contrary:

> Again, Oh, impious heedlessness! if anyone were to have
> the presumption to say of Christ's humiliation, Let us
> now forget all that has to do with His humiliation. Yet
> surely Christ's humiliation was not something which
> merely happened to Him (even though it was the sin of
> that generation that they crucified Him), something
> which happened to Him and perhaps would not have
> happened to Him in a better age. Christ Himself willed
> to be the humiliated and lowly one. Humiliation (the fact
> that it pleased God to be the lowly man) is therefore
> something He Himself has joined together, something He
> wills to have knit together, a dialectical knot which no
> one shall presume to untie, which indeed no one can un-
> tie before He Himself has untied it by coming again in
> glory.[8]

It is Jesus Himself who has chosen His state of degradation in order to become a sign of contradiction for people
and a dialectical knot. Kierkegaard describes people's reaction to this sign. Jesus, he says, makes His appeal: "Come
hither unto me, all ye" and yet nobody comes. Instead of
seeing, as one would expect, a horde of suffering creatures
accept the invitation, we see exactly the opposite—a mass
of people recoiling with fright.[9] The first effect produced
by the sign of contradiction is recoil. Jesus, the lowly man
who pretends to be God and who desires to help people, becomes an object of derision:

> That a man who makes such an appearance as that, a man
> who is shunned by everybody who has the least particle

150

of common sense in his noddle and has anything in the world to lose. . . . that He says, "Come hither to me!"— what an uninviting invitation! And then further: "All ye that labour and are heavy laden"—just as if people like that hadn't already enough troubles to bear, and then in addition would expose themselves to all the consequences of associating with Him. And finally: "I will give you rest." That caps the climax—He will help them! It seems to me that even the most good-natured of the scoffers who were actually His contemporaries might well say, "That is the very last thing He should undertake—to wish to help others when He Himself is in such a plight. It is as if a beggar were to notify the police that he had been robbed. . . ."[10]

But if men withdraw from Jesus, it is because He Himself wants to be an obstacle, a restraint which should stop people from accepting the invitation en masse and for the wrong reasons. Although Jesus appeals to all people, He "brings one to a halt by making it evident that it is not just such a simple matter, but really quite an awkward thing, to follow the invitation. . . ."[11] Jesus invites the people to come to Him, but no distinction can be made between the invitation and the inviter. And, He does not invite the public, but rather, He solicits each person privately and as an individual.[12] Jesus addresses Himself to the heart of each person, and He wants each to be converted through his own choice. It is precisely in choosing this state of degradation and in pleading ignominy that Jesus opens people's hearts. While being mocked, insulted, and crucified, Jesus loves His persecutors despite their insults, contempt, and persecution. In His lowly state He demonstrates sacrifice, and it is that meekness that expresses the sign of contradiction which will

make Christian faith flower in people's hearts. The self-
abnegation of Jesus reaches a point where it cannot be ig-
nored. It attracts people and leaves them the choice of taking offense or believing. In choosing suffering and cruci-
fixion, Jesus became the paradigm who teaches a suffering
love. If then Jesus states that He Himself is God, this is not
an idle word nor a direct pronouncement but an action, a
word tied to a life full of sacrifice which no human being
can bypass. Jesus is God *through* His lowliness, and His
misery appears *through* His sublime devotion. He is a sign
of contradiction whose aim is to make people Christians,
but by their own choice:

> But what does it mean "to draw unto Himself"? It means
> to draw unto Himself through a contradiction, through
> a choice, hence not immediately but mediately, so that
> the choice (as has been said) does not consist in choosing
> one or the other of the contraries, but in choosing a unity
> of two contraries, a thing that cannot be done immedi-
> ately. In view of this He cannot be said to *draw* only from
> on high, as though He were simply the highly exalted
> One and never had been anything else.[13]

It is for love that God became man, and it is through the
sufferings He inflicted upon Himself that He wants to teach
them true self-abnegation. The essential thing is for a man
to become Christian by his own choice, i.e., to choose self-
abnegation without being forced to do so. And it is precisely face to face with Jesus that he learns to do this. Man
needs a human teacher to instruct him in sacrifice, and it is
the lowliness of God which provides the example to follow.
Face to face with Jesus who suffers, man can choose Christianity, and choosing Christianity means renouncing the
finite world and self-esteem. For it is the fact that Jesus

loves His persecutors *in spite of everything* that softens a man and changes his hardened heart and his attachment to the finite world. Jesus as a sign of contradiction prepares people for this surrender.

Let us remember that Kierkegaard describes Jesus as the sign of contradiction in ways that are analogous to his description of profound humor. In fact, the two signs, Jesus and humor, resemble each other even though they are also different. Any indirect communication supposes two disparate qualitative opposites, and Jesus is this as well. Furthermore, the teacher of indirect communication is always incognito, and this is so even with Jesus. As Kierkegaard says, Jesus as a man is the incognito who is God Himself. In becoming a man, God is hidden in a human being. Just as indirect communication gives a distance to the learner, so is this exactly the effect produced by Jesus as a sign of contradiction. Initially His lowliness offends the learner. Nevertheless, there is a capital difference between Jesus and any other indirect communication.

The qualitative opposites deployed by the ironist or the humorist belong to the world of phenomena. Whether the matter in question is the union of the tragic and the comic, or unhappiness and happiness, the communication is always parasitic on the range of common things. But the designer of such a communication always keeps a distance from this world and is ever the objective and even disinterested witness of it. Flaubert does not become personally involved in the progress of his novel *Madame Bovary* and Kierkegaard allows existential possibilities to burst forth in his works of which he himself wants to be only a witness and a reader like others. But it is different with Jesus. Besides the indirect communication we have just spoken of, Kierkegaard recognizes another form of indirect communication:

But indirect communication can be brought about also in another way, by the relationship between the communication and the communicator. Whereas in the former case the communicator was left out of account, here he is a *factor* [my italics], but (be it noted) with a negative reflection.[14]

While every other master of indirect communication keeps his distance from his own words, Jesus Himself is His own communication. He Himself is the lowly man as well as God. He suffers, He has Himself crucified, and He dies; it is always He Himself. He is the one who is miserable, and again He is the one who loves and evinces love even for His persecutors. He does not talk these things; He is these things. Consequently there is no distance between the communication of Jesus and His actual life. He Himself is the union of lowliness and sublimity, or, as Kierkegaard says, He is a negative reflection in person, i.e., a union of contradictory opposites. In *Training in Christianity* and elsewhere, Kierkegaard constantly stresses that the words of Jesus are his very life, and that Christianity is not a doctrine but a life, an existential communication. Jesus does not want to teach something directly, for Christian communication does not communicate anything objective. On the contrary, it is renunciation—the recoil from objective phenomena— that Jesus wishes to communicate indirectly, and He does this through His own life, through His sacrifice of Himself.

There are other essential differences between Jesus and other indirect communications. In *Works of Love*, Kierkegaard compares Christian love to Socratic irony.[15] Speaking of Socrates and also of the Christian lover, he says:

That noble rogue [Socrates] had profoundly understood that the highest that one human being can do for another

is to make him free, to help him stand alone—and he had also understood himself in understanding this, that is, he had understood that if this is to be accomplished, the helper must be able to conceal himself in magnanimously willing his own destruction. He was, as he himself called himself, a midwife in a spiritual sense, and with every sacrifice he worked disinterestedly in this service—for the disinterestedness consisted simply in keeping hidden from the one helped how and that he was helped. . . . In such an understanding of help to another person there is agreement between the true lover and that noble rogue.[16]

Christian love as well as irony have the aim of freeing the other person, i.e., of making him renounce the immediate. The fact that the Christian loves his neighbor *despite everything*, has an effect upon the latter and makes him, in turn, renounce his attachment to the immanental world. Moreover, irony also provokes renunciation in the other person, though in its own fashion. There is, however, a difference between irony and Christian love: irony still trades on prideful superiority, while Christian love is a complete self-abnegation. The ironist likes to see himself as an aristocrat. He is proud of being able to free people and thus shows himself to be superior. That is why the ironist, as Kierkegaard says, sustains "an indescribable smile." We have furthermore seen that the humorist is attached to his capacities as well, although he constantly renounces the immediate. Laughing and smiling are a sort of auto-satisfaction that can be completely foreign to Christian love.

In addition, Christian love has its origin in the hidden nature and life of Jesus, and the range of this communication surpasses the range of any other indirect communication. The highest thing a man can do for another is to free

him, Kierkegaard tells us. That is all that a human teacher can accomplish through his indirect communication. He makes people draw away, creating in them an internal void which rids them of their objective burden. His indirect communication awakens negative self-reflection in them, and the activity of the communication ends with this energizing of self-reflection. On the other hand, the indirect communication of Jesus simultaneously provokes two things in man. In teaching love and total self-renunciation, it is engaged in an analogous sort of activity, though much more profound, namely, detachment from the finite. But the love that Jesus teaches is inseparably connected with Jesus Himself, with the person of Jesus, who practices renunciation in His life. To love in a Christian fashion is then to discover the existence of God in time. Jesus as indirect communication on the one hand makes men renounce the immediate, and on the other, has the effect of leading them through faith to being *qua* being, to being as positive determinant which Kierkegaard, as we have seen, calls "immediacy after reflection." What Jesus provokes in the believer are precisely the two movements which, according to Kierkegaard, were made by Abraham: on the one hand absolute resignation, and, on the other, repetition. Christianity, says Kierkegaard, is "an existential communication" and not a doctrine. It is in Christian faith that man attains transcendent existence and knows the basis and origin of all the world. It is during the moment that the absolute coming-out-of-oneself is produced, whereby man finds his transcendent origin. Man then becomes aware that the intrusive action of transcendent existence, the action which gives rise to the phenomenal world, is the action of God manifested in nature. Let us recall the passage in the *Journals* where Kierkegaard speaks of the "omnipotence" which creates "the visible total-

ity of the universe." God is manifested in nature at every moment, He is always a current presence. This is what Kierkegaard sees as part of the import of being "contemporaneous with Christ."

Jesus as a man is a phenomenon which has existed in history. He is certainly an objective fact as was Napoleon, for instance, or any other historical personage in the course of objective history. But we have seen that His historicity is equally possible to know, equally accessible to the capacities of any man anywhere; but Jesus as an historical personage cannot be the total object of faith. One does not need faith to recognize an historical fact, for it is enough to read historical research in this connection. The capacities immanent in all are enough for that. A study of history can only prove the ordinary historical existence of Jesus, not His real existence and nature which is of God:

> *Can one learn from history anything about Christ?* No. Why not? Because one can "know" nothing at all about "Christ"; He is the paradox, the object of faith, existing only for faith.[17]

> But what does that [history] prove? At the most it might prove that Jesus Christ was a great man, perhaps the greatest of all; but that He was . . . God—nay, stop there! The conclusion shall by God's help never be drawn.[18]

Any historical study can be directly communicated and as such it can never go beyond the purveyance of disinterested facts. That is why Kierkegaard derides any attempt aiming to "prove" Christianity by "proving" the historical existence of Jesus. Jesus as an historical phenomenon is only the object of a quantitative approximation which gathers historical details, and such an object cannot be the foundation on which eternal blessedness is to be built. The object

157

of faith is not Jesus as an historical "other," but Jesus as a
transhistorical "other" whose presence is always with us. As
an offense against reason, Jesus is not a simple phenomenon
but rather a sign of contradiction which necessarily attracts
people's attention. Man cannot avoid paying attention to
this sign, and face to face with it, he has only one alterna-
tive: to believe, or to take offense:

> . . . the God-Man exists only for faith; but the possibility
> of offense is just the repellent force by which faith comes
> into existence—if one does not choose instead to be
> offended.[19]

As a sign of contradiction, i.e., as an indirect communication, Jesus is a shock to people. We have seen that every indirect communication produces such a shock, and that this
shock or thrust makes people experience something unex-
pected and totally different. While every other indirect
communication leads to experiencing that transcendent in
an indirect manner, by creating a void in man, Jesus actually leads man to the externality. In the moment of faith
man attains the being *qua* being which is behind every phenomenon, and he does this in a positive fashion. But the
possibility of faith is linked closely with the possibility of
offense, for it is offense which attracts people and teaches
them love and renunciation. Contemporaneousness with
Christ is established through offense, through the thrust
which is evidence of the current presence of the "outside."
Kierkegaard reproaches his contemporaries for distorting
Christianity by eliminating the possibility of offense:

> With every word suggestive of the qualification God,
> with every act that bears this suggestion, the possibility
> of the offense is presented. In the situation of contempo-
> raneousness everybody will take notice of it. But in Chris-

tendom we have all become Christians without noticing
the least possibility of any offense. . . . yea, it would seem,
without even noticing that it is Jesus Christ Himself that
calls attention to the presence of the possibility of the
offense. . . .[20]

Being a sign of contradiction, Jesus attracts the attention
of people and teaches them to open their hearts to love. And
it is in this self-renunciation that man discovers the existence of God, and the contemporaneity of the Absolute. The
moment of faith and the new birth of man will never come
if one does not reduplicate in his own case the actual life of
Jesus, i.e., total self-renunciation and humiliation. The existence of God will not be revealed through objective historical accounts but only through what Kierkegaard calls
the "sacred history,"[21] which consists of actually obeying the
paradigm that Jesus is. To be a real Christian is to be a contemporary of Jesus, and one can become a contemporary
of Jesus only by modeling one's own life after Jesus' lowly
state:

> . . . Christ Himself willed to be the humble man, this is
> just what He would be accounted. Hence history must
> not incommode itself to do Him justice, nor must we with
> impious heedlessness fancy presumptuously that we
> know as a matter of course who He was. For no one
> *knows* that, and he who *believes* it must be contemporary
> with Him in His humiliation.[22]

Christendom, says Kierkegaard, has abolished Christianity. Instead of following the example given by Jesus, instead
of choosing renunciation and the fight against the everyday
world, Christians in the established order seek to prove the
existence of Jesus objectively and cognitively. And the
Christian church, instead of being a militant church pursu-

ing a battle against worldliness, considers itself a trium-
phant church in this world.[23] In June 1854, Kierkegaard
wrote the following passage in the *Journals*:

> The law of estrangement from God (and this story is the
> story of Christendom) is the following: everything that
> confirms the visible draws away from God. When there
> were no churches and the rare Christians gathered like
> fugitives and victims of persecution in the catacombs,
> God was closer to reality. Then churches were built—
> numerous, immense, and magnificent: God drew away
> to the same extent. For the proximity of God is inverse to
> that of the phenomenon, and this increase (of numerous
> churches, of magnificent churches) goes in the di-
> rection of the apparent, in regard to which God behaves
> inversely.[24]

These, then, are among Kierkegaard's comments on
Christianity as indirect communication. We have seen that
the aim of its maieutic communication is to lead man to the
moment of faith where he fathoms a new kind of transcendent existence. These observations lead us to the problem of
truth, for the moment of faith, according to Kierkegaard,
is the transition from error to truth, just as it is from non-
being to being.

In the chapter entitled "A Project of Thought" in *Philosophical Fragments*, Kierkegaard deals with the concept
"truth" by contrasting the attitudes of "Socratism" and
Christianity in this connection. Let us remember, however,
that in speaking of Socrates, Kierkegaard is actually presenting the outlook of Plato on the scope of the maieutic
system, and not what, in his opinion, is the attitude of Socrates himself.* What we actually have is a confrontation

---

* Author's note: This point is explained by Kierkegaard in a note
in *Postscript*, p. 184.

between the Platonic theory of recollection, using Socrates as example, and Christianity. We have already seen that Kierkegaard categorically rejects the possibility that recollection may bring a man to reality. According to him, that maieutic system can only have a negative result—that void created in the disciple as soon as he comprehends the teacher's aims and purposes. This is what the real Socratic relationship is, and it is exemplified also in Christianity. Referring to Jesus as a teacher, Kierkegaard writes:

> If the Teacher serves as an occasion by means of which the learner is reminded, he cannot help the learner to recall that he really knows the Truth; for the learner is in a state of Error. What the Teacher can give him occasion to remember is, that he is in Error. . . . In this manner the Teacher thrusts the learner away from him, precisely by serving as a reminder; only that the learner, in thus being thrust upon himself, does not discover that he knew the Truth already, but discovers his Error; with respect to which act of consciousness the Socratic principle holds, that the Teacher is merely an occasion whoever he may be, even if he is a God. For my own Error is something I can discover only by myself, since it is only when I have discovered it that it is discovered, even if the whole world knew of it before.[25]

Kierkegaard himself also believes that the maieutic relation typically ends in a self-discovery. However, this discovery does not lead the disciple to any positive content whatsoever. It only reminds the disciple that he is in "error." The teacher is an "occasion" which precipitates the disciple into acknowledging his ignorance. His presence "thrusts the learner away from him," awakens him, and makes him renounce that which he has heretofore considered truth. Socrates as well as Jesus are "occasions," which remind man of

his "error." But the effect of Jesus's communication surpasses even that of Socrates'. While "the highest that one
human being can do for another is to make him free," Jesus
accomplishes two things at one time. On the one hand, he
makes man open up by making him renounce the immediate through love. But on the other hand, he actually leads
him toward being *qua* being, toward the Absolute which
is the origin of all phenomena. That is why Jesus is not an
ordinary occasion according to Kierkegaard, but an essential occasion, which gives a man new birth by leading him
to his transcendent origin. Contrarily, Socrates and all other
human teachers can only achieve a negative result through
their communications. In the following two passages, Kierkegaard speaks of the import of the relationship between
Jesus and man:

> The Teacher is then the God himself, who in acting as an
> occasion prompts the learner to recall that he is in Error,
> and that by reason of his own guilt. But this state, the be-
> ing in Error by reason of one's own guilt, what shall we
> call it? Let us call it *Sin*.[26]

> In so far as the learner was in Error, and now receives
> the Truth and with it the condition for understanding it,
> a change takes place within him like the change from
> non-being to being. But this transition from non-being to
> being is the transition we call birth. Now one who exists
> cannot be born; nevertheless, the disciple is born. Let us
> call this transition the *new birth*. . . .[27]

Just as much evil is a human creation, so sin is constituted
by man only. The sinner is the person who shuts himself
into his own immanence and defiantly considers it his actuality. The domain of immanence is in itself error, for each
phenomenon rooting in it only hides transcendence from

man. In the moment of faith, God reveals transcendent existence to man, and it is at this moment that man realizes his fall. Truth and rebirth are connected with each other. Truth is essentially anchored in the relationship with God which reveals being *qua* being to man. And it is up to man to choose between liberty, being opened up to the good and the truth on the one hand, and error, being closed in, confined to evil and bondage, on the other.

In dealing with the question of truth, Kierkegaard, in *Postscript*, writes:

> Whether truth is defined more empirically, as the conformity of thought and being, or more idealistically, as the conformity of being with thought, it is, in either case, important carefully to note what is meant by being. . . . If being, in the two indicated definitions, is understood as empirical being, truth is at once transformed into a *desideratum*, and everything must be understood in terms of becoming; for the empirical object is unfinished and the existing cognitive spirit is itself in process of becoming. Thus the truth becomes an approximation whose beginning cannot be posited absolutely, precisely because the conclusion is lacking, the effect of which is retroactive.[28]

This excerpt notes two differing concepts of truth. On the one hand we have the classical concept, which considers truth to mark the correspondence between thought and the object. But on the other hand, Kierkegaard substitutes another concept which inheres and illumines his own philosophy. As ordinary consciousness does not encompass being *qua* being, one cannot suppose an agreement between thought and this being. As to consciousness itself, it cannot even voice the dichotomy between the subject and object.

As the finite is an integral part of consciousness itself, we can no longer speak of an object which is definitively given, distinguishable from the subject. Human consciousness is part of the phenomena to begin with, since it is a synthesis of the general and the particular which is constantly engaged in the process of becoming. The particular phenomenon emerges in consciousness and acquires a meaning there. But as the process of becoming makes phenomena emerge ceaselessly, consciousness is constantly changing, and this is equivalent to saying that the phenomenal world changes as well. Human consciousness can never get outside itself and know itself. It can only try to decipher emerging phenomena in order to approach "being" more and more closely, without, however, ever attaining it. Truth cannot therefore be a perfect agreement between thought and being, but only a *desideratum*, the goal of the process of infinite approximation. Kierkegaard replaces the classical definition of truth with another expressed in the famous sentence: "Truth is subjectivity." Truth, at least in morals and religion, is in the very process of becoming. In *Postscript*, Kierkegaard writes:

> For an objective reflection the truth becomes an object, something objective, and thought must be pointed away from the subject. For a subjective reflection the truth becomes a matter of appropriation, of inwardness, of subjectivity, and thought must probe more and more deeply into the subject and his subjectivity.[29]

The "object" is a kind of abstraction, an arbitrary fixing which congeals the continuous change by ascribing to it a conceptual finality. But such positivity and objectivity are speculative illusions which language and direct communication create. For in the self-reflective man, replete with a

negative consciousness, the phenomena are never summed up in objective givens. For the subjective thinker, the phenomenon is not an object, but only a sign. We have already seen that by "sign" Kierkegaard means "the negation of immediacy, or a second state of being different from the first." Objects, too, are in flux. The fact that the subjective thinker knows himself enables him to interpret the phenomena as signs. When he sees something green, for instance, even the green emerges in his consciousness. It is not a raw happening. When he is well practiced as a thinker the congruity between the phenomenon and his consciousness allows him usually to say he is seeing a tree. But since consciousness is the permissive ground and itself has a history, the subjective thinker knows the tentativeness of even the most objective of claims. It is not inconceivable that we may one day see a white tree or a triangular one, for example, and these will change our idea of what a tree is. On the other hand, the green phenomenon can be the sign of a tree, a plant, a bush, etc. But as concepts are the means of these fixings of the phenomena, the true Tree or the true Bush (i.e., the tree or bush as a definite given) is really a hidden object, subject to infinite approximation. It is only an alienated consciousness which tends to content itself with positive objects and to become completely opaque and completely self-certain.

Just as the subjective thinker learns to construe the phenomenon as a sign, so too does he use linguistic terms as signs. In *Works of Love*, Kierkegaard writes:

All human language about the spiritual, yes, even the divine language of Holy Scriptures, is essentially transferred or metaphorical language. This is quite in order for it corresponds to the order of things and of existence

165

since even though man is spirit from the moment of birth
he first becomes conscious as spirit later, and therefore
prior to this he has lived for a certain time within sensuous-psychic categories. The first portion of life shall
not, however, be cast aside when the spirit awakens. . . .
The first portion is taken over by spirit, and, thus used,
thus laid at the base, it *becomes transferred.* Therefore
the spiritual man and the sensuous-psychic man say the
same thing in a sense, and yet there remains an infinite
difference between what they say, since the latter does
not suspect the secret of transferred language, even
though he uses the same words, but not metaphorically.
. . . One in whom the spirit is awakened does not therefore leave the visible world. Although now conscious of
himself as spirit, he is still continually in the world of the
visible and is himself sensuously visible; likewise he also
remains in the language, except that it is transferred.
Transferred language is, then, not a brand new language;
it is rather the language already at hand. Just as spirit is
invisible, so also is its language a secret, and the secret
rests precisely in this that it uses the same language as the
simple man and the child but uses it as transferred.[30]

As long as man is not yet spirit, he is an immediate synthesis of the body and soul which, according to Kierkegaard, Adam in the state of innocence exemplifies. But in
becoming a spirit, man does not divest himself of the sen-
suous completely. He remains in the phenomenal world,
and he becomes even more sensitive to the phenomena in
it. However, as he learns a kind of detachment, he dares to
conceive even the world itself, not as a definite given, but
also as a sign. The phenomenon may be a sign sometimes of
one reality, sometimes of another; but man as a spirit is al-

ways ready to redefine what he considers to be a real object, since he well knows that an object is always an achievement and a conceptual determinant. The uncertainty and caution which characterize the subjective thinker do not allow him to take the phenomenon for what it is immediately, and just as he considers it a sign, he takes linguistic terms as signs too. Aware that terms cannot frame all of dialectical activity, he dares to use them in a figurative and transposed manner. For example, the verb "edify" has the immediate meaning of "construct" or "build." But the same verb, says Kierkegaard, is used in the Scriptures by way of transference: one finds the expression "love edifies" in it. The subjective thinker flexes language freely to express this or that immanent experience. And just as the meaning of a work of art does not rest only upon the medium that expresses it, so human immanence cannot be transmitted only by the contents of language but also by the manner in which it is used.

Being continually in the process of becoming, and actually living in the uncertainty and relativity that characterize the world, the subjective thinker transforms truth into an infinite approximation. Truth even becomes the goal of his own life, not only of this thought. In *Postscript*, Kierkegaard writes: *"An objective uncertainty held fast in an appropriation-process of the most passionate inwardness is the truth. . . ."*[31]

The more man intensifies his consciousness, the more an awareness of objective uncertainty increases in him. He becomes more detached from the deceptive positivity of objects, and he is thus opened to other activities which may help him to redefine the reality that he is and that he lives. Sensitive to this uncertainty, the subjective thinker commits himself to the quest for truth, and this quest only intensifies

the negativity, his needs and hunger, within his consciousness. Let us recall the passage in *Postscript* where Kierkegaard considers the inwardness of the Christian as "the
greatest possible." The quest for truth only broadens that
inwardness, but it does not resolve it into self-contentment
and self-exaltation.

The philosophy of Kierkegaard does not recognize the
existence of hypostatized essences of any sort. The concepts
that consciousness possesses are no more than the linguistic
determinants, coined from emerging phenomena. These
concepts change their meanings constantly, or rather, it is
necessary to change them in view of the qualitative nuances
which emerge unceasingly. According to Kierkegaard, Socrates knows neither "Beauty," "Virtue," nor "Man." In *Philosophical Fragments*, Kierkegaard praises the wisdom of
Socrates who admitted not really knowing whether he himself was a monster or had something divine in him.[32] Kierkegaard takes up this point in the *Journals*:

My whole existence is in fact the deepest irony. . . .

In what does the irony of Socrates lie? Does it lie in his
expression, his phrases and his words? No, such trivialities do not make a Socrates, though they be of a virtuosity
which constitutes speaking in an ironic fashion. No, his
entire existence was an irony, and it was the following:
While the whole population of his time, the young people, the merchants, etc., in brief all those thousands of
men were sure that they were men and that they knew
what "being a man" meant, Socrates ironically effaced
himself and concerned himself with the problem: What
is it to be a man. . . .

In relation to Christendom, irony has in it an additional

consideration which Socratic irony does not have. In Christendom, people imagine, not only that they are men (this is where Socrates stops), but also that they are something historically concrete, like the fact of being Christian. Socrates doubted that one was a man upon coming into the world. . . . For it is the ideality of what it is to be a man that concerned him, that was what he sought. But what would Socrates have thought if one had told him that at present people have become so perfect, that they have made such progress in non-sense, that today it has become reasonable to believe that an infant is almost born a Christian. . . .[33]

Socrates, says Kierkegaard in *Postscript*, "puts the question objectively in a problematic manner: *if* there is an immortality. . . . On this "if" he risks his entire life, he has the courage to meet death, and he has with the passion of the infinite so determined the pattern of his life that it must be found acceptable—*if* there is an immortality."[34] And like Socrates, Kierkegaard as a *philosopher* does not objectively apprehend eternal happiness nor what it means "to be a man." He must pursue these with his passions. One generally has the habit of projecting concepts on to the subject, but these concepts are only shadows of the phenomena and consequently have nothing stable in them. Only the believer comes to realize what man actually is, for God reveals to him that man is a sinner.[35] Consider this excerpt from *The Sickness unto Death:*

A self face to face with Christ is a self potentiated by the prodigious concession of God, potentiated by the prodigious emphasis which falls upon it for the fact that God also for the sake of this self let Himself to be born, became man, suffered, died. As was said in the foregoing,

"the more conception of God, the more self," so here it is true that the more conception of Christ, the more self. A self is qualitatively what its measure is. That Christ is the measure is on God's part attested as the expression for the immense reality a self possesses; for it is true for the first time in Christ that God is man's goal and measure, or measure and goal.—But the more self, the more intense the sin.[36]

The contact with transcendence which takes place at the "moment" reveals to man the true nature of what he is. The believer becomes aware that his life is cut off from its transcendent origin, that it is a fall. And the greater man's consciousness becomes, the more he becomes aware of the distance separating him from God. "The more self, the more intense the sin," says Kierkegaard. It follows that there is never an end to the struggle against the finite on which man's return to his transcendental origin depends. Man remains a sinner forever. But it is not less true for all that that even practical necessity leads men to even deeper alienation. For, throughout a lifetime the man himself gradually becomes another object—only a body.

Christianity aims to reinterpret the phenomenal world by transforming man into a subjectivity resembling God. God creates the phenomena, but He is not Himself one of these. He creates the world continually, but He does it, says Kierkegaard, while withdrawing and staying invisible. God is not an object, but pure subjectivity:

> God is pure subjectivity; there is no trace of anything objective in Him; for everything that possesses such objectivity thereby enters the realm of the relative.[37]

For man as well to become a subject requires that he relativize the phenomenal world around him. As we have seen,

this means that he must consider the finite only as a sign and not as spiritually accomplished. Although the practical exigencies of life constrain man to triviality, he must at the same time be ready to reinterpret what he takes to be his world. Our concepts are always "after the fact" in relation to emerging phenomena, and it is the task of the subjective thinker to renounce his objective certainty in order to seek the true meaning of our world and ourselves, as well as the intention of God, who created it. According to Kierkegaard, it is not inconceivable that the world is "a system—for God,"[38] but man knows nothing of this objectively. The world as an object will always remain a secret, to be known only by an approximation and conjecturally.

Returning to the problem of truth, Kierkegaard's definition—that truth is subjectivity—transforms the classical definition of truth into something negative and of lesser import. As the meaning that consciousness imparts to phenomena can only be relative, no invariant agreement can be established between consciousness and being *qua* being. The movement of approximation in which consciousness is engaged never arrives at a definitive and changeless result. This means that truth is the least possible fault, or the least possible alienation. But man cannot determine the sense of the world by himself. Through pride, disregard, or ignorance, he tends not to be aware of all the aspects and nuances of the things around him. He therefore needs God to awaken him from the state of alienation. What Kierkegaard means by "truth is subjectivity" is, therefore, basically the following: "Truth is inter-subjectivity."

The individualism expressed in Kierkegaard's philosophy has often been misunderstood. It has not been realized that this individualism can develop only in the bosom of human society. It is certainly true that society can also produce

alienation in man, but, on the other hand, the birth and evolution of subjectivity in man depends on the maieutic communication by which one man educates another. Even God,
the transhistorical other, provides a condition for the consciousness of his interlocutor, thus impelling him to detach
himself from the finite and transcend himself and the world.
It is precisely that negative condition which transforms man
into a truer subject and differentiates him from the animal
whose nature is characterized by a conglomeration of finite
and immediate needs. Negativity impels man not to be satisfied with the gratification of his immediate needs, and to
seek what is "other" than himself, until he attains transcendence through faith. But negativity in a man can be
maintained and intensified only by means of the stimuli provoked by other persons. The transhistorical God forces his
interlocutor to give up his false convictions and redefine the
world in which he lives. Whether what I am seeing at present is a tree, a mirage, or a hallucination depends also on
the confirmability and presence of others. Man's immanent
reality, the concepts therein formed, the moral and esthetic
appreciations prevalent in it—all of these are basically social products, for they are contributed and reconstituted by
social intercourse. In the *Journals*, Kierkegaard writes:

> When there is no earthquake, no eruption, no plague, no
> war, etc., to teach men the uncertainty of everything, the
> sermons of the pastors should do this service each day.
> Well, just try it![39]

Far from being interested in the question of how truth is
learned, Kierkegaard concerns himself with finding out how
ignorance is learned. What must be taught to man is precisely the awareness of failure. Again this cannot be done
directly. Man as a conscious being can never assimilate this

as a truth. God himself is truth and it is possible that for Him the world is a system. But man can know little objectively, and he can only approach truth by emulating Jesus' path of suffering. Jesus is truth, not as an objective truth but as a life in which the finite and the infinite are constantly synthesized. In the following two passages Kierkegaard deals with truth:

> Christ is the truth in such a sense that to *be* the truth is the only true explanation of what truth is. Hence one may ask an Apostle, one may ask a Christian, what truth is, and then the Apostle or the Christian will point to Christ and say, "Behold Him, learn of Him, He was the truth." That is to say, the truth, in the sense in which Christ was the truth, is not a sum of sentences, not a definition of concepts, etc., but a life. Truth in its very being is not the duplication of being in terms of thought. . . . No, truth in its very being is the reduplication in me, in thee, in him, so that my, that thy, that his life, approximately, in the striving to attain it, expresses the truth, so that my, that thy, that his life, approximately, in the striving to attain it, is the very being of truth, is a *life*, as the truth was in Christ, for He was the truth.[40]

> God has so arranged this existence that it is truly impossible to have a relation with truth without suffering. . . .[41]

Jesus teaches people, but again indirectly, that they are miserable offenders, and their awareness of this leads to a new kind of being for them. Jesus constantly renounces the ordinary and the finite and precisely thereby shows man the road to truth. This road begins for each man with the renunciation of the immediate. By inspiring love, Jesus teaches men a true social life in which they can struggle together against alienation from their true selfhood and

173

achievement. Man needs society in order to escape this alienation. Christian love aims, furthermore, to form a society in which people can help each other to become true subjects. The individualism expressed by Kierkegaard's philosophy is an attitude which can be formed only in the bosom of a Christian society, and for this reason, if no other, it is important to note that Kierkegaard did not want to leave the Danish church, though he criticized it incessantly. It is true that the brochure entitled "The Instant," which he published during the last year of his life, is a direct attack against the church. Although in writing this Kierkegaard departed from his own theory of indirect communication, that attack confirms his own observations on alienation. Alone, bitter, and without a friend among the leaders of the Danish church, he collapsed under the burden of his solitude. But it is not less true that for the greater part of his life Kierkegaard respected that church, always hoping that it would be a militant church and that its members would become active fighters against the world. Kierkegaard did not wish to live apart from the church and Christian society. He knew that solitude does not form subjectivity; it forms only an alienated man.

Our observations in this chapter have concerned Kierkegaard's reflection on Christianity as indirect communication. We have seen that Christianity is an existential communication aiming to transform man into spirit and make him acknowledge his transcendent origin. Christianity reveals to man what is truly in him—that he is fallen, a sinner; and it bids him to be born again in faith. The love of Jesus teaches man self-abnegation, but the moment of faith subsequently reveals transcendent existence to him. To live, from the Christian point of view, is to try to become subjective while believing in God and in the forgiveness of sin

174

which raises man from his fall. A passage from the *Journals* makes this clear:

Believing in the forgiveness of his sins is the decisive crisis through which man becomes spirit; he who does not believe this is not a spirit. In this lies the maturity of the spirit; in other words, all immediacy is lost. Not only is man incapable of anything by himself, but he can only harm. . . . The forgiveness of sins does not in fact focus on something in particular—as if one were not entirely good (that is childish; the child always asks pardon for a particular act . . .); no, on the contrary, it focusses not so much on particular acts as on the totality; it concerns our entire ego which is sinful and which perverts everything at the least contact. The man then who has in truth lived and now lives the experience of believing in the forgiveness of his sins has certainly become another man. Everything is forgotten, but it is not the same for him as for the child who, once pardon has been obtained, becomes essentially the same child again. No, he has grown older by an entire eternity; for from then on he is a spirit; all immediacy, his egoism, his egoistical attachment to the world and to himself are lost. From then on, to speak honestly, he is old, immensely old, but for eternity he is young.[42]

10.

The Historicity and Temporality of Consciousness

IN SPEAKING of the immanence of man, Kierkegaard hovers over three areas at once. According to him, man is the synthesis first of the finite and the infinite, then of the temporal and the eternal, and finally, of freedom and necessity.[1] It is the latter two contentions that are of interest here, and in considering them we shall see that the structure of consciousness of which we have spoken is a temporal one. Its character becomes more and more evident as man intensifies his inwardness while following the path which leads from the esthetic stage of life to the religious stage. It is in this last stage that the temporality of consciousness is completely evident, while in the esthetic stage it is often absent.

But a word about the temporality of consciousness is in order here. Several considerations are pertinent to the issue. For one thing, it is quite evident that Kierkegaard's view of the contents of the mind is in no way comparable to that of Henri Bergson, who argued that the thoughts and percepts are atemporal and static. Reality, he believed, is temporal and actually flows—it has a durational quality. But mental life and consciousness are like a strip of movie film in relation to the flow of events. That film, made up of still pictures, creates the illusion of motion by being run through the projector faster than the eye can discriminate.

So, Bergson said, the human mind is cinematographical. For all of the concern that Kierkegaard expends upon the differences between the finite and the infinite in respect to consciousness, he never phrases the difficulties in the manner of Bergson. The features of the mind—ideas, thoughts, etc.—are not eternal and atemporal, and the world outside of consciousness temporal and changing.

Instead, Kierkegaard's concern is with "how" a person takes his own temporal life! This means that the Danish thinker is concerned to show his reader that one's consciousness is subject to a kind of management and deployment. Consciousness is not a mental substance residing in the body. It is not a thing, not a divine essence, not describable as an object. Rather, consciousness is a feature of human behavior. But as a feature, it has—if we wish to use the noun "consciousness" again as a substantive but albeit somewhat figurative expression—such attributes as would make it atemporal in some instances and temporal in others. Here, however, the issue is whether a person does or does not have those affective and passional qualities that we have already noted. If he allows himself to become hopeful or if he dwells in his memories, then he has already, in virtue of hope and memory, temporalized his consciousness. The issue is, then, affectional and passional, not logical and ideational.

Volatilized in romantic abstractions and devoured by his moods, the estheticist is most often insensitive to time. Just as the esthetic consciousness does not describe a clear demarcation between the finite and the infinite, neither does it live in full awareness of past, present, and future. In the chapter entitled "The Unhappiest Man" in *Either/Or*, Kierkegaard describes an estheticist who is conscious neither of the present, nor of the past, nor of the future.[2] In him the

177

three aspects of time come together in a sort of obscure fusion where their distinctive characteristics are lost. Elsewhere in the same work, the estheticist says:

Time flows, life is a stream, people say, and so on. I do not notice it. Time stands still, and I with it. All the plans I make fly right back upon myself; when I would spit, I even spit into my own face.[3]

The time of which the estheticist is aware is like a crossroads where he has halted and is passing the time. The esthetic stage of life can thus be considered an atemporal stage. The estheticist has no hope, and therefore no future; he allows himself no regrets, and therefore the concept of the past is empty. All that is left is a "now." There are no lively temporal distinctions.

The result is that the estheticist has no historical consciousness; in other words, he does not live in a responsible historical fashion. His inward experiences are characterized by surprises and intermittent lapses, and the heights and depths of his changing moods do not shape an historical continuity. The estheticist, says Kierkegaard, has only an external history, and no internal history.[4] What the romantic poet actually traces is the conflict between the romantic soul of the hero and the external reality in which he lives. For while an historical account deals with the details and temporal development of events, romantic poetry is only interested in evanescent experiences in which romantic passion reaches its peak. The estheticist does not live within any historical continuity, for the esthetic stage of life becomes increasingly ahistorical as well as atemporal. The inward history of man appears only in the ethical stage in which consciousness, having become reflective, develops an inward continuity and temporal distinctions. The historical

"other," the other as a "future," appears in his consciousness, and the ethicist thus establishes his relationship with
his neighbor as well as with history. He flexes the world
now in a set of historical and temporal concepts. But they
are engendered by the new ethical earnestness that is his.

Since it is a synthesis of the finite and the infinite, the reflective consciousness is actually a synthesis of necessity and
freedom as well. However, by "necessity" Kierkegaard does
not mean logical necessity. Criticizing Hegel, he writes:

> Thus when a person entitles the last section of his Logic
> "Reality," he thereby gains the advantage of appearing
> to have already reached by logic the highest thing, or, if
> one prefers to say so, the lowest. The loss is obvious nev-
> ertheless, for this is not to the advantage either of logic
> or of reality. Not to that of reality, for the contingent,
> which is an integral part of reality, cannot be permitted
> to slip into logic. It is not to the advantage of logic, for if
> logic has conceived the thought of reality it has taken into
> its system something it cannot assimilate, it has antici-
> pated what it ought merely to predispose.[5]

Logic, since it is a conceptual and abstract science, is not
the province of the real. Neither the actual and transcendent real nor the phenomenal real can be enfolded by a logical system that is always characterized by necessity. Necessity is a feature of the self-contained nature of logical discourse, in virtue of which the conclusion is given as soon as
the premises are formulated. It is possible, says Kierkegaard, that the world is a system for God, but man knows
nothing of this objectively. Even for the believer, who has
already come to realize their origin, phenomena are hap-
hazard, for he cannot accurately know therefrom the will
and intention of God who created them. Kierkegaard criti-

cizes, even attacks, Hegel for having introduced logic into the real, or the real into logic, for they belong to two different orders, one being temporal and the other atemporal. Logical concepts are not, therefore, transcripts of the world-experience.

In this connection let us note that while Kierkegaard is critical of Hegel, he maintains that formal logic is the only valid kind. He refuses to recognize the possibility of any other kind of logic, and the mediation between logic and reality of which Hegel speaks seems to him a "chimera" which is designed to abolish the law of contradiction. Therefore, to be human, Kierkegaard insists, requires a synthesis within a man of two contradictory determinants which no logical mediation can reconcile. On the contrary, Kierkegaard wishes to teach us actually to live that disparateness instead of trying to project it into logic itself.

Although logical necessity does not foreshadow one's temporal conscious activity, consciousness is subject to another sort of impingement, that of chance or arbitrariness. The emergence of a phenomenon, though not determined or foreseen by a logical system, must be acknowledged. The particular phenomenon confronts one whether one likes it or not. One turns one's head and sees the world. The chance, or arbitrariness, that, according to Kierkegaard, characterizes the real is on the one hand apparently fortuitous, and on the other, a constraint imposed upon us. In *The Sickness unto Death*, Kierkegaard writes:

> Just as finitude is the limiting factor in relation to infinitude, so in relation to possibility it is necessity which serves as a check. When the self as a synthesis of finitude and infinitude is once constituted, when already it is potentially,* then in order to become it reflects itself in the

* Author's note: Kata dynamin. In the text it is written in Greek.

medium of imagination, and with that the infinite possibility comes into view. The self is potentially just as possible as it is necessary; for though it is itself, it has to become itself. Inasmuch as it is itself, it is the necessary, and
inasmuch as it has to become itself, it is a possibility.

Now if possibility outruns necessity, the self runs away
from itself, so that it has no necessity whereto it is bound
to return—then this is the despair of possibility. The self
becomes an abstract possibility which tries itself out with
floundering in the possible, but does not budge from the
spot, nor get to any spot, for precisely the necessary is the
spot; to become oneself is precisely a movement at the
spot. To become is a movement from the spot, but to become oneself is a movement at the spot.[6]

The meeting with each finite phenomenon is a meeting
with facticity. The finite emerges in us at every moment and
thereby helps to constitute us. This facticity, this necessity
of always "being-there" (Dasein, in Heidegger's term) is evidence of the healthy and nonalienated state of consciousness. We have already seen that to the extent that man intensifies his inwardness he becomes more and more receptive to the world. Contrarily, the estheticist tries to ignore
the finite by attenuating himself in abstract dreams; his consciousness is intransitive and does not acknowledge what is.
The finite endlessly impedes the estheticist in his flights of
imagination, and this is the cause of his melancholy moods.
But the moment man leaves the esthetic stage and becomes
a new kind of subjective, he learns to yield to the presence
of facts which, in turn, constitute him anew in the world.
He then becomes what we ordinarily would term "a realist."
This healthy state of consciousness in fact consists of recognizing determinants around him. In the excerpt quoted
above and in its sequel, Kierkegaard attributes the despair

produced in most of us to the lack of being thus "necessi-
tated" and goaded into self-consciousness.

Such necessities, however, are not the sole determinant
of the reflective consciousness, for it is a synthesis of the
finite and the infinite, of necessity and freedom. Since the
reflective consciousness perceives the world also in order
to detach itself, it thereby becomes free to affirm itself. It
engenders some things freely too. The negation of the par-
ticulars permits the exercise of the synthesizing consciousness which now brings the past to bear upon the present.
We then become aware of what we already are, and that we
cannot deny being this. Of course, what we have then is a
consciousness of failure and limitation; for compared with
the infinite number of ways of being, what we are already
can only be a limitation of them. We could have been something other than what we at present are, thanks to the fact
that we are free. But, on the other hand, the negation of the
current finitude makes man free to come out of himself in
order to become himself, i.e., to accept the new circumstances that arise. For the subjective thinker, facticity, i.e.,
the necessity of "being there" as a fact, is not something
done once and for all, for he himself is constantly in the
state of becoming. We have seen that in the movement of
becoming, what is called objective has no finality. The character of the man is itself waiting and opening toward the future, and through this future, one can establish himself ever
anew. By receiving the world while detaching himself from
it, man opens himself toward other phenomena which will
help him to understand and redefine his present life. Moreover, facticity and the past suppose a kind of familiarity
with the world. Man already knows more or less what a tree
is, and it is in terms of this "already," of this past, that he
tries to identify other phenomena that emerge. Certainly

the future may have something new in it, but we always receive it with our past, while at every moment we are also
a facticity modified by the phenomenon which is currently
emerging. Thus we become new persons who extend themselves toward the future and incorporate the past at the
same time. A readiness for the future and a regression toward the past occur in an enriched consciousness and transform it into a free person.

In *Philosophical Fragments*, Kierkegaard maintains that
the past is not subject to logical necessity, for every historical event is a becoming. He writes:

> What has happened has happened as it happened; in this
> sense it does not admit of change. But is this immutabil-
> ity identical with the immutability of the necessary? The
> immutability of the past consists in the fact that its actual
> "thus" cannot become different; but does it follow from
> this that its possible "how" could not have been realized
> in a different manner? The immutability of the necessary,
> on the contrary, consists in its constant relating itself to
> itself, and in its relating itself to itself always in the same
> manner, excluding every change. It is not content with
> the immutability that belongs to the past, which as we
> have shown is not merely subject to a dialectic with re-
> spect to a prior change from which it emerges, but must
> even suffer a dialectic with respect to a higher change
> which annuls it. (Repentance, for example, which seeks
> to annul an actuality.)[7]

The necessity which relates to itself, and always in the
same way, is the logical necessity in which nothing changes.
The past is not subject to this sort of necessity. The only
necessity which Kierkegaard recognizes in regard to the
past is the plain "givenness" of historical events. However,

there seems to be something contradictory in the excerpts we have just quoted. We learn at the end of the excerpt that the invariable "thus" is quite variable. But the contradiction is only apparent. For by the "thus" of an historical event, Kierkegaard means that at its emergence the historical phenomenon could have been different. Anything historical could once have been otherwise. For example, I read a book which teaches me that Napoleon is an historical fact. I read the book and look at a picture, and here is Napoleon emerging in me as a possible. The confrontation with the phenomenon is always a current event. It is now that I learn something about Napoleon for the first time in my life. In that context, a Napoleon is imposed upon me and will always be imposed upon anybody who reads history. But on the other hand, Napoleon as an historical fact changes constantly, for each piece of historical research and every additional detail changes the ideas that I have about him. Thus, like any phenomenon, Napoleon is both variable and invariable, simultaneously both a "how" and a "thus." His status in the consciousness of readers is a contraint, a "thus," but his characteristics develop from his relationship to other phenomena that are subsequently to be known, as well as those already existing. So it is with our common consciousness. We face the past and the future at once, and every man seeks to understand both his present state and every historical fact in virtue of this complexity. The historian takes a new look at the past that he is studying; and the past, in thus becoming a present, is also a synthesis of necessity and freedom. But that synthesis is always new and is always being redone in lively minds.

The analysis of the historicity of consciousness, of course, shows what the temporal character of conscious activity means. But here temporality is not quite what we make of

it in our ordinary conceptions of time. It is generally believed that one "advances" in time in a linear fashion, always facing the future and leaving the past behind. In *The Concept of Dread*, Kierkegaard criticizes this linear view of time:

> When time is correctly defined as infinite succession, it seems plausible to define it also as the present, the past and the future. However this distinction is incorrect, if one means by it that this is implied in time itself; for it first emerges with the relation of time to eternity and the reflection of eternity in it. If in the infinite succession of time one could in fact find a foothold, i.e., a present, which would serve as a dividing point, then this division would be quite correct. But precisely because every moment, like the sum of the moments, is a process (a going-by) no moment is a present, and in the same sense there is neither past, present, nor future. If one thinks it possible to maintain this division, it is because we *spatialize* a moment, but thereby the infinite succession is brought to a standstill, and that is because one introduces a visual representation, visualizing time instead of thinking it.[8]

The linear conception of time is a convenient conceptual scheme but it does not stand up. For either time is a continuum and has no articulation, or it has articulation and is then not a continuum but rather a line which is arbitrarily divided. The linear conception of time is another abstraction, and like any abstraction, it is deceiving. As a matter of fact, the tendency to spatialize time stems from the faults which characterize the alienated consciousness. The moment one believes that one possesses time as named facts, one tends to arrange them according to the linear conception of time. On the other hand, while negativity is main-

tained in consciousness, its every current moment relates to the other dimensions of time, in the same dialectical fashion that the emerging finite relates to the synthesized consciousness. Time must also be lived, and one must develop a kind of flexible personal consciousness, involving regrets, repentance, hope, and anticipation to do it justice. One needs not just concepts, but new features of one's behavior, new feelings and emotions, in order to incorporate time correctly, albeit noncognitively.

All conceptual articulations of time are based on the inward experience whose point of departure is always the present, the place where one can find a foothold. The present is born through the intrusive activity of transcendent existence which makes a phenomenon emerge, and it is then that features of time are brought together in a dialectical union. The temporality of consciousness is created in "the moment," i.e., in the moment of contact between transcendence and immanence:

> The instant is that ambiguous moment in which time and eternity touch one another, thereby positing *the temporal*, where time is constantly intersecting eternity and eternity constantly permeating time. Only now does that division we talked about acquire significance: the present, the past, and the future.[9]

Temporality, i.e., even time as an articulated ensemble, is produced in the moment in which the eternal qualities impinge upon the subject. Now, in the excerpt just quoted, the term "eternity" designates two different things. The eternity which "touches" time is God, who creates the synthesis of the temporal and the eternal. We thus have two kinds of eternity, one a positive and transcendent determinant, and the other a negative and immanent one. In *Works*

of Love, Kierkegaard notes: "[Possibility appears when the eternal gets into touch with the eternal which is within a human being in Time.]"[10]

The moment is an ambiguous moment, like a glance of the eye (Øjeblikket), but it is at the same time "the fullness of time."[11] This fullness is actually captured by a consciousness in which the three dimensions of time intersect one another. In *The Concept of Dread*, Kierkegaard writes:

> The concept around which everything turns in Christianity, the concept which makes all things new, is the fullness of time, is the instant as eternity, and yet this eternity is at once the future and the past.[12]

In the moment of faith, the Christian relates to an historical fact of the past, to the Incarnation. But he relates to it, not cognitively, but passionally, in a lived contemporaneousness with Christ, and thereby he finds eternal blessedness. In this passional temporality which is typical of the religious consciousness, the temporal "after" and "before" characteristics of the linear conception of time disappear. The three dimensions of time manifest are simultaneously in it, related reciprocally, and thus establish the dialectical character of consciousness. We have already seen, in considering Kierkegaard's remarks on the religious stage, that the immanence of the believer is a "continuous meanwhile."[13] The more profound immanence is, the more its dialectical temporality is manifested. Kierkegaard stresses, however, that "the moment" is given only for the spirit, for only the spirit experiences noncognitively the transcendence. So long as man is not yet a believer, the true character of temporality is either completely, or, at best, partially hidden. For example, for Adam, who is no more than an immediate being, the eternal still means a distant future or

involves a vague expectation of some indeterminate thing.[14] On the other hand, for the Christian who really lives no longer threatened by time, the eternal catches up the present, the past, and the future—they become equally his and God's.

Compared with the linear conception of time, the Christian's notion of temporality is eternal youth. The generally held concept of old age derives from a fearing thought which considers human life in worldly terms. It supposes that life has a beginning and an end which are birth and death. This ordinary thought spatializes time, and as a result it fixes the phenomenal world in "objects" or in positive "facts" which are arranged in space. However, it is death which actually shows the fallacy of objective thought, for death can never be apprehended by it. Death can never be a positive "fact" for us. It is an unknown possibility, an objective uncertainty, and an enigma which we can never decipher while we are alive. Death not only expresses the limitations of objective thought, but actually teaches man to become subjective. One must learn to fear it, to face it, to overcome it altogether. In *Postscript*, Kierkegaard states that subjectivity develops in the reflection on the possibility of death.[15] Death occasions, if we do not forget it or try to obliterate any reflection about it at all, a whole variety of affective and passional, emotional and feelingful subjective traits. These, too, are more appropriate than objective thoughts for such an occurrence; and they enrich our consciousness. The presence of faith gives us a victory over death that is our transcendence; but this comes only as a gift of God.

Our thoughts about death remain objectively uncertain and serve to intensify the awareness of our limitations. One generally conceives of death either as a rupture which in-

188

terrupts the continuity of life, or as nothingness. However, such conceptions do not lessen the uncertainty in regard to death, but rather increase it. And it is precisely this uncertainty which teaches man not to keep too tight a hold of the temporal things, and thus helps him to become spirit. For the Christian, death has no objective and definitive existence. The moment of faith brings him face to face with Jesus, and this presence frees him from the past as well as from the future. Face to face with God, and awaiting eternal blessedness, the believer retains his youthful spirit eternally. In renouncing the immediate, a man ages, as Kierkegaard says, "by an eternity." From the objective and worldly point of view, he is already dead, but "for eternity he is young."

Our object in this chapter has been to consider the new characteristics of human consciousness. We have seen that the structure of consciousness is a temporal one in which the three dimensions of time are bound up in a dialectical knot. Historical existence which binds man to his past and to the future has its origin in the temporal awareness which is characteristic of human consciousness. The historicity of consciousness is part of the subjective history of man, which is emancipated in the ethical stage of life, and then becomes intensified in the religious stage. In this last stage, the historicity of consciousness is dramatically related anew to a historical figure who is simultaneously the Absolute in time. But, so, too, does a believer have his own temporal concerns vanquished altogether by discovering God, the Eternal, who while being vanquished in time is the victor over it.

11.

Conclusion

THE STRUCTURE and behavior of consciousness was described in the beginning of this work, and demonstrated by our analysis of the philosophical production of Kierkegaard. The conclusions deriving from this study remain to be stated.

Human consciousness, if it is not alienated and misled, is an infinite movement of becoming. This movement is expressed in man's fundamental aspiration to attain a transcendental world in which he hopes to find his own Self, the One, the Absolute. The search for the Absolute has always been the interest of metaphysics, and Kierkegaard, like many other philosophers before and after him, takes part in this search. The philosophy of Kierkegaard, however, heralds the end of metaphysics. Philosophical reflection, since it is an immanent activity of man, can never attain that reality which is beyond the phenomenal world. The Absolute and being *qua* being are the objects of faith; and, in fact, only the believer can bridge the abyss which separates the phenomenal world from transcendent being. In the exaltation of the moment of faith, the believer looks down and recapitulates the fall of man in the finite world. Only the believer is a spirit living simultaneously in the three dimensions of human consciousness, and only the believer, not the philosopher, attains such transcendence.

Kierkegaard came to understand the differences between

the possibilities and the transcendent real, via the moments of faith which he experienced in his life. It should be noted that Kierkegaard did not consider himself a philosopher. In his works, he does not present what he wants to say by means of a philosophical theory. He stresses that he is a religious writer, but also a poet-dialectician who wants to "make people aware"; and he considers his production only an edifying discourse. By drawing readers to the new possibilities, he wants to lead them to discover themselves as such, so that they will explore the possibilities thereof and lend themselves to the moment of faith in which the real is manifest. The philosophical work of Kierkegaard is an art, an indirect communication which does not establish anything objective, and which, on the contrary, makes the reader withdraw from objectivity by plunging him into inward reflection and new forms of subjectivity. It is true that in his works Kierkegaard formulates some language about his main philosophical principle on the difference between the phenomenal and the transcendental realities. But his pronouncements on the subject do not pretend to be objective description and, according to Kierkegaard himself, they have only a suggestive and eliciting value.

Just as Kierkegaard rejects metaphysics, he likewise objects to any philosophical attempt to formulate an absolute, autonomous, and rational ethics. Ethical science, he says in the introduction to *The Concept of Dread* is no more than an ideal kind of science seeking to impose itself on human reality without taking into account that sin which is an essential limit of this reality.[1] As a matter of fact, neither morality as an assemblage of practical maxims and of customs nor the science of psychology can take cognizance of sin. Since it is a transcendent category, sin, as well as the concept "sin," is revealed only in the moment of faith in

which man fathoms the difference separating himself from the transcendent God. And it is only the Christian ethics (Kierkegaard also calls it "the ethical-religious") that embraces the reality of sin. This kind of ethics assumes the fall of man, and teaches mankind to love one another and help one another to become free. But just as Christianity is not a doctrine, so Christian ethics does not aim to formulate any practical maxims. It seeks only to form a certain attitude in a man which must precede and condition the formulation of such maxims. This attitude is Christian love. In Christian love, consciousness attains the highest degree of openness toward others. Of course this openness affects that social activity which should also augment the well-being of mankind. Nonetheless, this latter activity is only a consequence of Christianity and not its aim. The primary goal of Christianity is to form an attitude, a new consciousness called "love," in man. Speaking of mercifulness, Kierkegaard says:

> Does mercifulness consist in giving hundreds of thousands to the poor? No. Is it mercifulness to give a halfpenny to the poor? No. Mercifulness is *how* it is given.[2]

The charity and alms given to the poor are not the chief requirements of Christianity, but rather the result of it. For what is important in Christianity is first and foremost the basic attitude and quality of consciousness of man which empowers mercy, abnegation, and love. It is enough to love one's neighbor, and the rest will come of itself.

Since it is based on Christianity, the philosophy of Kierkegaard does not aim to formulate an immanental ethics. And it is not in the ordinary ethical terms that Kierkegaard judges human behavior. According to him, good is the development and unfolding of a man's life by love and denial in the presence of God. Conversely, evil is a closing-in upon

oneself and a kind of self-conceit. Good and evil denote two human attitudes, one authentic and one nonauthentic, and it is up to man to choose one of them. In order to become authentic and truly human, one must first recognize his limits by seeing all that he is. The true man bows to the evidence presented by the finite as a confrontation; and he chooses to be himself, to be what he is at every moment. On the other hand, the estheticist is indifferent to his own limitations and idle thoughts penetrate him like streams of air and blow him away. Such an alienated man does not choose his facticity or himself; facticity chooses him and manipulates him mechanically. The true man, however, consciously chooses his own facticity and assumes responsibility for it. However, at the same time, his choice is a choice that retracts, since he learns that he is not bound to the finite, but can resign himself and even free himself from it and thus open himself to other and new potentials. He constantly renews himself by tearing away from his immediacy as well as from the self-esteem, prejudices, and false convictions rooted therein. The ethical choice of which Kierkegaard speaks requires a kind of exile. In order to avert further alienation from his true subjectivity and selfhood, a man must constantly tear himself from his limits until in faith he becomes aware of the fact that the entire phenomenal world is groaning unto the day of deliverance. Christianity recalls man to his transcendental origin by making him apprehend the fact that the finite world suffers from the same fall as he does. Then it is up to every man to struggle against the finite and against his own further separation for the fulfillment of his glory that is his God-given privilege and goal.

Authenticity and nonauthenticity are the "either/or" which Kierkegaard presents to his readers, and it must be

stressed that according to him it is a deep social education which will engender a deeper truth and subjectivity for him. The subtle shifts and spurts provoked by the indirect communications of other men, the great teachers, are absolutely indispensable to the spiritual evolution of man. Only in the bosom of society can man become a new and free subject, for he needs daily contact with others in order to win over the world. The relationship with others and with society lends a new quality and characteristic to his consciousness, and this relationship, which begins to develop in the ethical stage of life, finally provides even the criterion of the truth which is the new life and the new subjectivity.

Kierkegaard addresses himself to educators and clergymen and proposes that an indirect communication is the means of intensifying the learner's subjectivity. Without maieutic educators, no man will be able to become either a good man or, especially, a Christian. According to Kierkegaard, Christian society is the *conditio sine qua non* of Christianity, and no one can be simultaneously a Christian and a hermit.

WORKS CITED

WITH the permission of the publishers, the quotations from Kierkegaard in the present volume are taken from the following editions:

The Concept of Irony, tr. Lee Capel. New York: Harper and Row, 1966.

Either/Or, Volume I, tr. David F. Swenson and Lillian Marvin Swenson; Volume II, tr. Walter Lowrie. Princeton: Princeton University Press, 1944.

Fear and Trembling and *The Sickness unto Death*, tr. Walter Lowrie. Princeton: Princeton University Press, 1954.

Repetition, tr. Walter Lowrie. Princeton: Princeton University Press, 1941.

Philosophical Fragments, tr. David Swenson, rev. tr. Howard V. Hong. Princeton: Princeton University Press, 1962.

The Concept of Dread, tr. Walter Lowrie. Princeton: Princeton University Press, 1957.

Stages on Life's Way, tr. Walter Lowrie. Princeton: Princeton University Press, 1940.

Concluding Unscientific Postscript, tr. David F. Swenson and Walter Lowrie. Princeton: Princeton University Press, 1941.

The Present Age and "Two Treatises," tr. Walter Lowrie. London and New York: Oxford University Press, 1940.

Works of Love, tr. Howard V. and Edna Hong. New York: Harper and Row, 1962.

The Point of View, including *Two Notes about "the Individual"* and *On My Work as an Author*, tr. Walter Lowrie. London and New York: Oxford University Press, 1939.

Training in Christianity, tr. Walter Lowrie. Princeton: Princeton University Press, 1944.

Works Cited

For Self-Examination and *Judge for Yourselves!* and Three Discourses, 1851, tr. Walter Lowrie. Princeton: Princeton University Press, 1944.

A few quotations are translated from the Danish edition of the Journals:

Søren Kierkegaards Papirer, 2nd edition, ed. P. A. Heiberg, V. Kuhr, and E. Torstig. Copenhagen: Gyldendal, Nordisk Forlag, 1909-1946.

One quotation is translated from:

Søren Kierkegaards Samlede Værker, 3rd edition, ed. A. B. Drachmann, J. L. Heiberg, and H. O. Lange. Copenhagen: Gyldendal, Nordisk Forlag, 1963.

NOTES

INTRODUCTION

1 See the article of R. Jolivet in *Kierkegaard Symposion.*
2 See Selected Bibliography.

CHAPTER 1.

1 *The Sickness unto Death*, p. 146.
2 *The Concept of Dread*, p. 37.
3 *Philosophical Fragments*, p. 50.
4 *The Sickness unto Death*, p. 146.

CHAPTER 2.

1 *Either/Or*, Vol. I, pp. 252-53.
2 *Either/Or*, Vol. II, p. 189.
3 *Repetition*, pp. 42-43.
4 *Philosophical Fragments*, p. 51 (note).
5 *Repetition*, p. 34.
6 Ibid., pp. 3-4.
7 Ibid., p. 6.
8 Ibid., pp. 4-5.
9 Ibid., p. 94.
10 Ibid., pp. 68-69.
11 Ibid., p. 74.
12 Ibid., p. 78.
13 Ibid., p. 156.
14 Ibid., p. 92.
15 Ibid., p. 15.
16 Ibid., p. 114.
17 Ibid., pp. 155-57.

18 *Journals*, IV A 107.
19 *Either/Or*, Vol. I, pp. 74-75.
20 *Either/Or*, Vol. II, p. 159.
21 *Either/Or*, Vol. I, p. 22.
22 *Either/Or*, Vol. II, p. 170.
23 Ibid., p. 152.
24 *Either/Or*, Vol. I, the chapter called "The Rotation Method."
25 Ibid., p. 17.
26 Ibid., p. 18.
27 *Repetition*, p. 79.
28 *Either/Or*, Vol. II, p. 150.
29 Ibid., p. 143.

CHAPTER 3.

1 *Either/Or*, Vol. II, p. 181.
2 *Repetition*, p. 114.
3 *Either/Or*, Vol. II, p. 150.
4 Ibid., p. 212.
5 Ibid., p. 216.
6 Ibid., pp. 208-09.
7 Ibid., pp. 181-82.
8 *Postscript*, p. 285.
9 *Journals*, X2 A 439.
10 *Either/Or*, Vol. II, pp. 218-19.
11 Ibid., p. 216.
12 *Postscript*, p. 151.
13 *Either/Or*, Vol. II, p. 180.
14 *Journals*, X2 A 428.
15 *Fear and Trembling*, p. 59.
16 *Journals*, XI2 A 436.
17 *The Concept of Dread*, p. 99 (note).
18 Ibid., p. 113.

Notes

19 Ibid., p. 106.
20 *Postscript*, p. 230.
21 *Fear and Trembling*, p. 59.
22 Ibid., p. 48.
23 Ibid., pp. 51-52.
24 *Repetition*, p. 94.
25 *Fear and Trembling*, p. 60.
26 Ibid., p. 92.

CHAPTER 4.

1 *Postscript*, p. 495.
2 Ibid., p. 494.
3 Ibid., pp. 516-17.
4 *The Concept of Dread*, p. 12.
5 *Samlede Værker*, Vol. XIX, p. 258.
6 *Journals*, X2 A 328.
7 *Journals*, VII A 181.
8 *The Sickness unto Death*, p. 224.
9 *The Concept of Dread*, p. 71.
10 *Fear and Trembling*, p. 38.
11 Ibid., p. 57.
12 *Postscript*, p. 494.
13 *The Sickness unto Death*, p. 250.
14 *The Concept of Dread*, p. 45.
15 *The Sickness unto Death*, p. 238.
16 *Journals*, X2 A 134.
17 *Postscript*, p. 339.
18 *Journals*, X2 A 354.
19 *Philosophical Fragments*, p. 46.

CHAPTER 5.

1 *Postscript*, pp. 497-98.
2 Ibid., p. 495.
3 Ibid., p. 498.
4 Ibid., pp. 364-65.
5 Ibid., p. 363.
6 *Philosophical Fragments*, p. 91.
7 *Postscript*, p. 469.

8 Ibid., p. 272.
9 Ibid., p. 353.
10 Ibid., pp. 489-92.
11 Ibid., p. 402.
12 Ibid., p. 404.
13 *Works of Love*, pp. 257-58.
14 Ibid., pp. 26-27.
15 *Philosophical Fragments*, p. 59.
16 *Works of Love*, p. 34.
17 Ibid., p. 37.
18 Ibid., pp. 64-65.
19 Ibid., pp. 80-81.
20 Ibid., p. 77.
21 Ibid., p. 40.
22 Ibid., p. 52-53.
23 Ibid., p. 58.
24 Ibid., p. 333.
25 Ibid., p. 38.
26 Ibid., pp. 64-65.
27 Ibid., p. 64.
28 Ibid., p. 181.
29 Ibid., part 2, ch. 9.
30 *Postscript*, pp. 506-07.
31 Ibid., p. 507.

CHAPTER 6.

1 *Judge For Yourselves!*, p. 115.
2 *The Sickness unto Death*, p. 169.
3 Ibid., pp. 166-67.
4 *The Present Age*, p. 3.
5 Ibid., p. 45.
6 *Postscript*, p. 174.
7 *The Concept of Dread*, pp. 124-25.
8 *The Present Age*, pp. 19-20.
9 *Judge For Yourselves!*, p. 129.
10 *The Present Age*, pp. 48-49.
11 *The Concept of Dread*, p. 85.
12 *Journals*, VI A 145-50.
13 *Either/Or*, Vol. I, pp. 74-75.
14 *Either/Or*, Vol. II, pp. 114-15.
15 *Works of Love*, p. 30.

16 *The Concept of Dread*, p. 111.
17 Ibid., p. 118.
18 Ibid., p. 122.
19 Ibid., p. 110.
20 Ibid., p. 38.
21 Ibid., p. 37.
22 Ibid., p. 38.
23 Ibid., p. 40.
24 Ibid., p. 38.
25 *Stages on Life's Way*, see the chapter called "Letter to the Reader."
26 *The Concept of Dread*, p. 121.
27 *Journals*, XI¹ A 209.

CHAPTER 7.

1 *Journals*, IV A 49.
2 *Postscript*, p. 115; see also *Journals*, VIII² B 83.
3 *Postscript*, p. 126.
4 Ibid., p. 70.
5 *Training in Christianity*, pp. 124-25.
6 Ibid., p. 124.
7 Ibid., pp. 124-25.
8 Ibid., pp. 132-33.
9 *Postscript*, p. 71.
10 Ibid., p. 491.
11 *The Concept of Irony*, p. 264.
12 *Training in Christianity*, p. 139.
13 *The Concept of Irony*, p. 266.
14 *Postscript*, p. 450.
15 Ibid., p. 78.
16 Ibid., p. 73.
17 *The Point of View*, pp. 54-55.
18 *The Concept of Irony*, p. 77.
19 Ibid., p. 222.
20 Ibid., p. 265 and pp. 341-42.
21 *Journals*, IV A 161.
22 *The Present Age*, pp. 49-51.
23 *Postscript*, p. 73.
24 Ibid., p. 74.

CHAPTER 8.

1 *Repetition*, p. 3.
2 *Journals*, VIII² B 83.
3 *Postscript*, pp. 75-76.
4 *Postscript*, p. 551.
5 *Journals*, X¹ A 510.
6 *Postscript*, p. 243.
7 *Samlede Værker*, Vol. IV, p. 102.
8 Ibid., p. 163.
9 Ibid., p. 209.
10 Ibid., p. 263.
11 *Postscript*, pp. 546-47.
12 *The Point of View*, p. 34.
13 *Postscript*, p. 69.
14 *The Point of View*, pp. 40-41.
15 Ibid., pp. 39-40.
16 *Postscript*, p. 316.
17 *Works of Love*, p. 23.

CHAPTER 9.

1 *Journals*, VIII A 42.
2 *Journals*, VII A 139.
3 *Training in Christianity*, pp. 26-27.
4 Ibid., p. 124 (esp. note 2).
5 Ibid., p. 134.
6 Ibid., p. 40.
7 Ibid., p. 107.
8 Ibid., p. 36.
9 Ibid., p. 25.
10 Ibid., pp. 41-42.
11 Ibid., p. 43.
12 Ibid., p. 16.
13 Ibid., p. 161.
14 Ibid., p. 133.
15 *Works of Love*, pp. 257-58.
16 Ibid., pp. 257-58.
17 *Training in Christianity*, p. 28.
18 Ibid., p. 29.
19 Ibid., p. 122.
20 Ibid., pp. 103-04.

[21] Ibid., p. 26.
[22] Ibid., p. 36.
[23] Ibid., pp. 204-05.
[24] *Journals*, XI² A 51.
[25] *Philosophical Fragments*, p. 17.
[26] Ibid., p. 19.
[27] Ibid., p. 23.
[28] *Postscript*, p. 169.
[29] Ibid., p. 171.
[30] *Works of Love*, pp. 199-200.
[31] *Postscript*, p. 182.
[32] *Philosophical Fragments*, p. 46.
[33] *Journals*, XI¹ A 188-89.
[34] *Postscript*, p. 180.
[35] *Philosophical Fragments*, pp. 19-23.
[36] *The Sickness unto Death*, pp. 244-45.
[37] *Journals*, XI² A 54.
[38] *Postscript*, p. 107.
[39] *Journals*, VI A 138.
[40] *Training in Christianity*, pp. 200-01.
[41] *Journals*, XI¹ A 353.
[42] *Journals*, VIII A 673.

CHAPTER 10.

[1] *The Sickness unto Death*, p. 146.
[2] *Either/Or*, Vol. I, p. 184.
[3] Ibid., p. 20.
[4] *Either/Or*, Vol. II, p. 113.
[5] *The Concept of Dread*, p. 9.
[6] *The Sickness unto Death*, pp. 168-69.
[7] *Philosophical Fragments*, p. 95.
[8] *The Concept of Dread*, pp. 76-77.
[9] Ibid., p. 80.
[10] *Works of Love*, p. 241.
[11] *Philosophical Fragments*, p. 22.
[12] *The Concept of Dread*, p. 81.
[13] *Postscript*, p. 469.
[14] *The Concept of Dread*, p. 81.
[15] *Postscript*, p. 151.

CHAPTER 11.

[1] *The Concept of Dread*, p. 15.
[2] *Works of Love*, p. 302.

SELECTED BIBLIOGRAPHY

ENGLISH STUDIES:

Collins, James. *The Mind of Kierkegaard*. Chicago: Henry Regnery Co., 1953.

Croxall, T. H. *Kierkegaard Commentary*. New York: Harper & Row, 1956.

Diem, Hermann. *Kierkegaard's Dialectic of Existence*. London: Oliver and Boyd, 1959.

Henriksen, Aage. *Kierkegaard Studies in Scandinavia*. Copenhagen: Munksgaard, 1951.

Holmer, P. L. "Kierkegaard and The Truth," unpub. diss., Yale University, 1945.

Johnson, Howard A. and Niels Thulstrup. *The Kierkegaard Critique*. New York: Harper & Brothers, 1962.

Jolivet, R. *An Introduction to Kierkegaard*. New York: E. P. Dutton, 1952.

Lowrie, W. *Kierkegaard*. New York: Harper & Brothers, 1962.

Rohde, P. *Søren Kierkegaard*. New York: Humanities Press, 1963.

Roos, Heinrich. *Søren Kierkegaard and Catholicism*. Westminster, Md.: Newman Press, 1954.

SCANDINAVIAN BOOKS AND ARTICLES:

Bejerholm, L. *Meddelelsens Dialektik*. Copenhagen: Lund, 1962.

Henriksen, Aage. *Kierkegaards Romaner*. Copenhagen: Gyldendal, Nordisk Forlag, 1954.

Holm, S. *Søren Kierkegaards Historiefilosofi*. Copenhagen: Bianco Lunos Bogtrukkeri, 1952.

Jansen, F. J. Billeskov. *Studier i Søren Kierkegaards Literære Kunst*. Copenhagen: Rosenkilde og Bagger, 1951.

Selected Bibliography

Løgstrup, K. E. *Opgør med Kierkegaard.* Copenhagen: Gyldendal, 1967.

Malantschuk, G. og Søe N. H. *Søren Kierkegaards Kamp mod Kirken.* Copenhagen: Munksgaard, 1956.

Malantschuk, G. *Dialektik og Eksistens hos Søren Kierkegaard.* Copenhagen: Hans Reitzels Forlag, 1968.

Rubow, P. V. *Goldschmidt og Kierkegaard.* Copenhagen: Gyldendal, Nordisk Forlag, 1952.

————. *Kierkegaard og Kirken.* Copenhagen: Gyldendal, Nordisk Forlag, 1955.

Schousboe, J. *Om Begrebet Humor hos Kierkegaard.* Copenhagen: Arnold Busk, 1925.

Welter, C. *Grundtvig og Søren Kierkegaard.* Copenhagen: Gyldendal, Nordisk Forlag, 1952.

Kierkegaardiana. Publication of the Søren Kierkegaard Selskabet, ed. Niels Thulstrup. Copenhagen: Munksgaard, 1955-1969.

Kierkegaard Symposion. Copenhagen: Orbis litterarum, 1955.

FRENCH STUDIES:

Grimault, M. *Kierkegaard par lui-même.* Paris: Le Seuil, 1963.

Hohlenberg, J. *Søren Kierkegaard.* Paris: Albin Michel, 1956.

Mesnard, P. *Le vrai visage de Kierkegaard.* Paris: Beauchesne et ses Fils, 1948.

Stucki, P. A. *Le Christianisme et l'histoire d'après Kierkegaard.* Basel: Verlag für Recht und Gesellschaft, 1963.

Wahl, J. *Etudes Kierkegaardiennes.* Paris: Vrin, 1938.

Kierkegaard Vivant, Colloque organisé par l'Unesco a Paris. Paris: Gallimard, 1964.